Everyday Blessings for Women

Everyday Blessings for *Women*

365 DEVOTIONS

TYNDALE
MOMENTUM®

A Tyndale nonfiction imprint

Visit Tyndale online at tyndale.com.

Tyndale, Tyndale's quill logo, *Tyndale Momentum,* and the Tyndale Momentum logo are registered trademarks of Tyndale House Ministries. Tyndale Momentum is a nonfiction imprint of Tyndale House Publishers, Carol Stream, Illinois.

Everyday Blessings for Women: 365 Devotions

Previously published in 2005 as *The One Year Mini for Women* by Tyndale House Publishers under ISBN 978-1-4143-0617-9.

General editors: Ronald A. Beers, Linda Taylor

Contributing editors: Rebecca Beers, Amy Mason, Christopher Mason

Contributing writers: V. Gilbert Beers, Ronald A. Beers, Brian R. Coffey, Jonathan Farrar, Jonathan Gray, Shawn A. Harrison, Sandy Hull, Rhonda K. O'Brien, Douglas J. Rumford

Designed by Libby Dykstra

Edited by Linda Schlafer and Susan Taylor

For information about special discounts for bulk purchases, please contact Tyndale House Publishers at csresponse@tyndale.com, or call 1-855-277-9400.

Library of Congress Cataloging-in-Publication Data
A catalog record for this book is available from the Library of Congress.

ISBN 979-8-4005-0088-6

Printed in the United States of America

30	29	28	27	26	25	24
7	6	5	4	3	2	1

Happy New Year

It's a brand-new year. Is it really possible for me to get a fresh start?

God's Response

Great is his faithfulness; his mercies begin afresh each day.
Lamentations 3:23

Do not despise these small beginnings, for the LORD rejoices to see the work begin.   *Zechariah 4:10*

TODAY BEGINS A BRAND-NEW YEAR, and God rejoices when you are able to see today—and every day—as a new beginning. Each new day gives you new opportunities to know God better. God renews his mercies to you every single day. Don't be burdened by yesterday's (or last year's!) failures or regrets. Instead, let today be a fresh new beginning to a fresh new year.

God's Promise

I am sure that God, who began the good work within you, will continue his work until it is finally finished on that day when Christ Jesus comes back again.
Philippians 1:6

New Beginnings

The year is new, but I still feel like the same woman I was yesterday. How do I get a new start?

God's Response

Those who become Christians become new persons. They are not the same anymore, for the old life is gone. A new life has begun! *2 Corinthians 5:17*

WHERE ARE YOU IN YOUR SPIRITUAL LIFE? Is Jesus your Savior? If so, then you are already a new person, and your new life has begun. Perhaps you're not sure about this, or maybe Jesus was once part of your life but has not been so recently. To really get a new start, commit or recommit to a relationship with Jesus. Look forward to this new year of walking with the Lord.

God's Promise

The one sitting on the throne said, "Look, I am making all things new!" *Revelation 21:5*

Forgiveness and Cleansing

I want to start life anew by being forgiven and cleansed. Will God truly do that?

God's Response

I will give you a new heart with new and right desires, and I will put a new spirit in you. I will take out your stony heart of sin and give you a new, obedient heart. *Ezekiel 36:26*

ASK JESUS TO FORGIVE YOUR SINS and to cleanse you from the inside out. With a clean new heart, you will also enjoy a new relationship with God. Will God truly do that? Yes! That's why he allowed his Son, Jesus, to die—so that you could be cleansed and forgiven. He's just waiting for you to ask.

God's Promise

"Come now, let us argue this out," says the LORD. "No matter how deep the stain of your sins, I can remove it. I can make you as clean as freshly fallen snow. Even if you are stained as red as crimson, I can make you as white as wool." *Isaiah 1:18*

Setting Goals

Everyone makes New Year's resolutions.
What are some goals I should set for the coming year?

God's Response

If we are faithful to the end, trusting God just as firmly as when we first believed, we will share in all that belongs to Christ.   *Hebrews 3:14*

Live in such a way that God's love can bless you.
Jude 1:21

AS YOU THINK ABOUT GOALS for the year, a good place to begin is with a commitment to apply your faith to your life and become more confident in what you believe. When you make these goals, you'll find that many other issues in your life will fall in line.

God's Promise

Take delight in the LORD, and he will give you your heart's desires.   *Psalm 37:4*

The Importance of Goals

Why are goals important?

God's Response

I run straight to the goal with purpose in every step.
1 Corinthians 9:26

Look straight ahead, and fix your eyes on what lies before you. Mark out a straight path for your feet; then stick to the path and stay safe. Don't get sidetracked; keep your feet from following evil.   *Proverbs 4:25-27*

GOALS GIVE US DIRECTION. You may have a lot of goals for different areas of life (including those New Year's resolutions you made), but make following God your primary, overarching goal. You do not know what the year ahead will bring, so setting that goal will give you purpose and keep you from straying away from God regardless of what life throws at you.

God's Promise

We can make our plans, but the LORD determines our steps.   *Proverbs 16:9*

More like Jesus

One of my goals is to be more like Jesus.
What kinds of goals did Jesus have?

God's Response

Even I, the Son of Man, came here not to be served but to serve others, and to give my life as a ransom for many. *Mark 10:45*

I brought glory to you here on earth by doing everything you told me to do. *John 17:4*

JESUS SOUGHT TO PLEASE and give glory to his Father in everything he did. That goal shaped the way he lived every day and helped him to serve others in every interaction. As you face each day of this new year, ask yourself two questions: Will my plans for today please God? Will I be serving others today? This will help you decide how to spend your time and make you more like Jesus.

God's Promise

He guides me along right paths, bringing honor to his name. *Psalm 23:3*

Right Choices

This new year is bringing some new choices and options. How can I make the right decisions?

God's Response

Oh, that you would choose life, that you and your descendants might live! Choose to love the LORD your God and to obey him and commit yourself to him, for he is your life. *Deuteronomy 30:19-20*

I have hidden your word in my heart, that I might not sin against you. *Psalm 119:11*

With many counselors, there is safety. *Proverbs 11:14*

LOVE AND OBEY THE LORD IN YOUR CHOICES. Listen continually to God's voice in his Word to help you discern the right direction for your life. Weigh carefully the advice of reliable counselors.

God's Promise

You will keep on guiding me with your counsel, leading me to a glorious destiny. *Psalm 73:24*

God's Guidance

How does God guide my decision-making?

God's Response

Who are those who fear the LORD? He will show them the path they should choose.   *Psalm 25:12*

Learn to be wise, and develop good judgment. Don't forget or turn away from my words.   *Proverbs 4:5*

God is working in you, giving you the desire to obey him and the power to do what pleases him.   *Philippians 2:13*

PRAY FOR THE DESIRE TO seek God's guidance and then to follow it. When you do, you will be able to make decisions that please him. God does not play games with you. He wants to give you guidance, not hide his will from you. Ask for his help, and then learn to hear him when he speaks.

God's Promise

Seek his will in all you do, and he will direct your paths. *Proverbs 3:6*

Tough Decisions

What if the "right" decision is the hardest one?

God's Response

Shadrach, Meshach, and Abednego replied, "O Nebuchadnezzar, we do not need to defend ourselves before you. If we are thrown into the blazing furnace, the God whom we serve is able to save us. He will rescue us from your power, Your Majesty. But even if he doesn't, Your Majesty can be sure that we will never serve your gods or worship the gold statue you have set up." *Daniel 3:16-18*

THE RIGHT DECISION MAY NOT always be the safest or the easiest one, at least in the short run. God will always do what is eternally right in your life, even though your decision might be a difficult one. Ask him to give you peace and protection as you follow his will.

God's Challenge

Trust in the LORD with all your heart; do not depend on your own understanding. . . . Don't be impressed with your own wisdom. Instead, fear the LORD and turn your back on evil. *Proverbs 3:5, 7*

My Worth

Does God really care about me and my life?
Why would he pay attention to me?

God's Response

God created people in his own image; God patterned
them after himself; male and female he created them.
Genesis 1:27

We are God's masterpiece. He has created us anew in
Christ Jesus, so that we can do the good things he planned
for us long ago.   *Ephesians 2:10*

GOD MADE YOU IN HIS OWN IMAGE, so he must value
you highly! You are his treasure, his masterpiece.
Your soul is so valuable to God that he sent his Son to
die for you. God cares about your life and wants to share
every moment of every day with you.

God's Promise

The LORD keeps watch over you as you come and go,
both now and forever.   *Psalm 121:8*

The Future

I'm setting goals and planning for my future, but our world is in a lot of turmoil. How can I face such uncertain times?

God's Response

Jesus Christ is the same yesterday, today, and forever. *Hebrews 13:8*

Don't worry about tomorrow. *Matthew 6:34*

God has reserved a priceless inheritance for his children. It is kept in heaven for you. *1 Peter 1:4*

YOU CAN FACE AN UNCERTAIN FUTURE because you have an unchanging God who loves and guides you. Don't waste time worrying about what-ifs. Take your concerns and uncertainties to God in prayer. No matter what the future of this earth holds, you can be sure that heaven will be perfectly free of problems and worries.

God's Promise

[Jesus said,] "Here on earth you will have many trials and sorrows. But take heart, because I have overcome the world." *John 16:33*

Heavenly Riches

What does it mean that God promises heavenly riches? Can I really believe that?

God's Response

That is what the Scriptures mean when they say, "No eye has seen, no ear has heard, and no mind has imagined what God has prepared for those who love him." *1 Corinthians 2:9*

YOU DON'T HAVE TO FEAR THE FUTURE. God's promises about heaven are as certain as all of his other promises. Being confident in God's promise of eternal life gives you courage and hope in your life now, and it changes the way you make choices every day. God has an eternal future planned for you that is far better than you can even imagine! Live today as though you truly believe that, and see how your perspective changes.

God's Promise

[Jesus replied,] "In the future you will see me, the Son of Man, sitting at God's right hand in the place of power and coming back on the clouds of heaven." *Matthew 26:64*

A Future with God

What other promises has God made about my future with him?

God's Response

When he comes we will be like him, for we will see him as he really is. *1 John 3:2*

He will remove all of their sorrows, and there will be no more death or sorrow or crying or pain. For the old world and its evils are gone forever. *Revelation 21:4*

YOU WILL ONE DAY BE LIKE CHRIST. You will not be equal to him in power and authority, but you will be like him in character and perfection, for there will be no sin in those God welcomes into heaven. You will never be in pain or experience sorrow, and evil will be gone forever.

God's Promise

The seventh angel blew his trumpet, and there were loud voices shouting in heaven: "The whole world has now become the kingdom of our Lord and of his Christ, and he will reign forever and ever." *Revelation 11:15*

Tomorrow

I know I can trust God for my eternal future, but what about the future that will be here tomorrow?

God's Response

"I know the plans I have for you," says the LORD. "They are plans for good and not for disaster, to give you a future and a hope." *Jeremiah 29:11*

You saw me before I was born. Every day of my life was recorded in your book. Every moment was laid out before a single day had passed. *Psalm 139:16*

G OD HAS PLANS FOR YOUR LIFE—plans he made before you were born. He knows what tomorrow holds, and he promises to go through it with you, so you can anticipate each new day with joy and hope. Perhaps tomorrow you will see God's plan for you more clearly than ever before.

God's Promise

We know that God causes everything to work together for the good of those who love God and are called according to his purpose for them. *Romans 8:28*

Things in my life aren't always rosy. How can trusting God's plan for my future help me live today?

God's Response

The LORD says, "I will guide you along the best pathway for your life. I will advise you and watch over you." *Psalm 32:8*

Our present troubles are quite small and won't last very long. Yet they produce for us an immeasurably great glory that will last forever! *2 Corinthians 4:17*

AS A HEAVEN-BOUND FOLLOWER OF JESUS, put heaven and earth in perspective. Here, you will probably live for less than a hundred years. In heaven, one hundred million years will still be just the beginning. Amazingly, God has determined that how you live during your short time on earth will prepare you for heaven. Wondering what unique role God has planned for us in eternity gives meaning to our troubles and adversity today.

God's Promise

For you who fear my name, the Sun of Righteousness will rise with healing in his wings. And you will go free, leaping with joy like calves let out to pasture. *Malachi 4:2*

When I'm Afraid

With so much change and instability in the world, I'm afraid. What can help me?

God's Response

All who listen to me will live in peace and safety, unafraid of harm.   *Proverbs 1:33*

Anyone who listens to my teaching and obeys me is wise, like a person who builds a house on solid rock. *Matthew 7:24*

WHEN YOU BUILD YOUR LIFE on God's truth, you have a solid foundation that will not crack under the world's pressures. When you are a Christian, your safety and security are based on the assurance that God is with you. Without him, you stand alone. With him, you can face life with great courage.

God's Promise

He set my feet on solid ground and steadied me as I walked along.   *Psalm 40:2*

Security

Can God help me feel secure about the future?

God's Response

Don't worry about anything; instead, pray about everything. . . . If you do this, you will experience God's peace, which is far more wonderful than the human mind can understand.   *Philippians 4:6-7*

Nothing in all creation will ever be able to separate us from the love of God.   *Romans 8:39*

GOD WILL HELP YOU FEEL SECURE about the future if you trust him. Security comes from allowing the peace of God to calm you through prayer. The most powerful security in the world is knowing that nothing can separate you from God's love.

God's Promise

I give them eternal life, and they will never perish. No one will snatch them away from me, for my Father has given them to me, and he is more powerful than anyone else. So no one can take them from me.   *John 10:28-29*

Safety

How does God provide security?
Can he really make me feel safe?

God's Response

The LORD is a shelter for the oppressed, a refuge in times of trouble.   *Psalm 9:9*

Have mercy on me, O God, have mercy! I look to you for protection. I will hide beneath the shadow of your wings until this violent storm is past.   *Psalm 57:1*

G OD PROMISES TO HOLD you securely, to be your shelter, refuge, and place of protection. No matter how the storms of life batter you, you are eternally secure with God. Nothing can ever separate you from his eternal presence. To feel safe, run to him.

God's Promise

God is our refuge and strength, always ready to help in times of trouble. So we will not fear, even if earthquakes come and the mountains crumble into the sea. Let the oceans roar and foam. Let the mountains tremble as the waters surge!   *Psalm 46:1-3*

Trust

I am reading the promises from the Bible.
How can I trust that God will do what he says?

God's Response

I am trusting you, O LORD, saying, "You are my God!"
Psalm 31:14

I pray that Christ will be more and more at home in your hearts as you trust in him. May your roots go down deep into the soil of God's marvelous love.   *Ephesians 3:17*

TRUSTING GOD IS AN ONGOING process based on a personal relationship with him. When you know him, you will love him. The more you love him, the more you will trust him. As your roots grow down deeply into him, you will find him to be completely worthy of your trust.

God's Promise

When you believed in Christ, he identified you as his own by giving you the Holy Spirit, whom he promised long ago. The Spirit is God's guarantee that he will give us everything he promised.   *Ephesians 1:13-14*

Trustworthiness

What makes God trustworthy?

God's Response

He passed in front of Moses and said, "I am the LORD, I am the LORD, the merciful and gracious God. I am slow to anger and rich in unfailing love and faithfulness." *Exodus 34:6*

This truth gives them the confidence of eternal life, which God promised them before the world began—and he cannot lie. *Titus 1:2*

Those who know your name trust in you, for you, O LORD, have never abandoned anyone who searches for you. *Psalm 9:10*

YOU CAN TRUST GOD BECAUSE he always tells the truth. Nothing he has said in his Word, the Bible, has ever been proven wrong or false. He specifically created you in order to have a relationship with you for all eternity. If God says he loves you—and he always tells the truth—you can rest in the assurance that he is trustworthy.

God's Promise

Your unfailing love will last forever. Your faithfulness is as enduring as the heavens. *Psalm 89:2*

Promise Keeper

Does God always keep his promises?

God's Response

[Joshua said,] "Soon I will die, going the way of all the earth. Deep in your hearts you know that every promise of the LORD your God has come true. Not a single one has failed!" *Joshua 23:14*

[Solomon] prayed, "O LORD, God of Israel, there is no God like you in all of heaven and earth. You keep your promises." *2 Chronicles 6:14-15*

Without wavering, let us hold tightly to the hope we say we have, for God can be trusted to keep his promise. *Hebrews 10:23*

G OD ALWAYS KEEPS HIS PROMISES. Joshua and King Solomon experienced this, and you can too. You can trust God to keep all of his promises to you.

God's Promise

As for God, his way is perfect. All the LORD's promises prove true. He is a shield for all who look to him for protection. *Psalm 18:30*

Well-Placed Trust

I've trusted people and been hurt.
What makes trusting God different?

God's Response

It is better to trust the Lord than to put confidence in people. It is better to trust the Lord than to put confidence in princes. *Psalm 118:8-9*

Cursed are those who put their trust in mere humans and turn their hearts away from the Lord. . . . But blessed are those who trust in the Lord and have made the Lord their hope and confidence. *Jeremiah 17:5, 7*

GOD IS PERFECT. While it is good and necessary to trust others, God is the only One you can trust completely. You can have complete assurance that what he says is true and that what he does is reliable. People are not perfect and will sometimes let you down, but God will never fail you.

God's Promise

God will surely do this for you, for he always does just what he says, and he is the one who invited you into this wonderful friendship with his Son, Jesus Christ our Lord. *1 Corinthians 1:9*

True Trust

How do I know if I am truly trusting God?

God's Response

Taste and see that the LORD is good. Oh, the joys of those who trust in him!   *Psalm 34:8*

You will keep in perfect peace all who trust in you, whose thoughts are fixed on you! Trust in the LORD always, for the LORD GOD is the eternal Rock.   *Isaiah 26:3-4*

When I am afraid, I put my trust in you.   *Psalm 56:3*

IF YOU ARE TRULY TRUSTING GOD, you will experience joy, peace, and confidence. When you give God control in a situation, you don't have to be anxious or afraid.

God's Promise

Those who trust in the LORD are as secure as Mount Zion; they will not be defeated but will endure forever. *Psalm 125:1*

Life's Purpose

How do I find true purpose in life?

God's Response

I take joy in doing your will, my God, for your law is written on my heart.   *Psalm 40:8*

Here is my final conclusion: Fear God and obey his commands, for this is the duty of every person. *Ecclesiastes 12:13*

PURPOSE IN LIFE COMES from knowing God and doing his will. The ultimate goal in life is not to achieve the goals you want, but to do what God has planned for you to do. God created you for a purpose and promises to fulfill his intentions in your life when you work with him.

God's Promise

I cry out to God Most High, to God who will fulfill his purpose for me.   *Psalm 57:2*

Special Purpose

Does God have a special purpose for me?

God's Response

Don't copy the behavior and customs of this world, but let God transform you into a new person by changing the way you think. Then you will know what God wants you to do, and you will know how good and pleasing and perfect his will really is. *Romans 12:2*

You didn't choose me. I chose you. I appointed you to go and produce fruit that will last, so that the Father will give you whatever you ask for, using my name. *John 15:16*

G OD HAS A GENERAL PURPOSE and a specific purpose for you. If nothing else, you have been chosen by God to let the love of Jesus shine through you to make an impact on others. More specifically, God has given you spiritual gifts and wants you to use them to make a unique contribution in your sphere of influence. The more you fulfill your general purpose, the more clear your specific purpose will become.

God's Promise

God knew his people in advance, and he chose them to become like his Son. *Romans 8:29*

Find and Fulfill

How can I discover my purpose and fulfill it?

God's Response

Dear brothers and sisters, I plead with you to give your bodies to God. Let them be a living and holy sacrifice—the kind he will accept.　*Romans 12:1*

My dear brothers and sisters, be strong and steady, always enthusiastic about the Lord's work, for you know that nothing you do for the Lord is ever useless. *1 Corinthians 15:58*

DISCOVERING GOD'S PURPOSE begins with your whole-hearted commitment to knowing God and his Word. God promises to make his will known to you as you make yourself available to him. When you commit yourself to fulfilling God's purpose for your life, the Lord promises that your life will be fruitful.

God's Promise

Let God transform you into a new person by changing the way you think. Then you will know what God wants you to do, and you will know how good and pleasing and perfect his will really is.　*Romans 12:2*

What should be my highest priority?

God's Response

Jesus replied, "The most important commandment is this: . . . Love the Lord your God with all your heart, all your soul, all your mind, and all your strength." *Mark 12:29-30*

Israel, what does the LORD your God require of you? He requires you to fear him, to live according to his will, to love and worship him with all your heart and soul, and to obey. *Deuteronomy 10:12-13*

WHEN GOD IS AT THE CENTER of your life, you will make your relationship with him your highest priority. You will long to spend time in prayer and in reading the Bible. Your thoughts will often turn to God. You will want to please him and obey him. The more you love God, the more your heart will long to be closer to his.

God's Challenge

Wherever your treasure is, there your heart and thoughts will also be. *Luke 12:34*

Right Priorities

How can I develop the right priorities?

God's Response

Solomon replied, . . . "Give me an understanding mind so that I can govern your people well and know the difference between right and wrong. For who by himself is able to govern this great nation of yours?"   *1 Kings 3:6, 9*

Jesus replied, "The most important commandment is this: . . . You must love the Lord your God with all your heart, all your soul, all your mind, and all your strength." *Mark 12:29-30*

WHEN LOVING GOD IS your first priority, all your other priorities will fall in order. You will be surprised at how clear life becomes when you ask God to prioritize your day.

God's Promise

Trust in the LORD with all your heart; do not depend on your own understanding. Seek his will in all you do, and he will direct your paths.   *Proverbs 3:5-6*

God's Will

*What are some things I should do to discover
God's will for my life?*

God's Response

If you want to know what God wants you to do—ask
him, and he will gladly tell you. He will not resent your
asking.   *James 1:5*

The LORD grants wisdom!   *Proverbs 2:6*

Oh, that we might know the LORD! Let us press on to
know him! Then he will respond to us.   *Hosea 6:3*

ACTIVELY SEEK GOD'S WILL through prayer and
Scripture reading and in conversation with mature
believers and reliable advisors. God promises that he will
respond to you. You will become more discerning about
your daily circumstances.

God's Promise

We can be confident that he will listen to us whenever we
ask him for anything in line with his will.   *1 John 5:14*

My Calling

How do I know what my calling is?

God's Response

Your word is a lamp for my feet and a light for my path.
Psalm 119:105

My life is worth nothing unless I use it for doing the work
assigned me by the Lord Jesus.   *Acts 20:24*

THE FIRST STEP IN KNOWING your calling is to get to
know God intimately through his Word. He will
show you what to do. When God gives you a specific
calling, it fills your thoughts and energizes you so that you
will long to pursue it wholeheartedly.

God's Promise

May the God of peace make you holy in every way,
and may your whole spirit and soul and body be kept
blameless until that day when our Lord Jesus Christ
comes again. God, who calls you, is faithful; he will
do this.   *1 Thessalonians 5:23-24*

Abilities

I'm really good at certain things.
Can God use those abilities as I serve him?

God's Response

Well done, my good and faithful servant. You have been faithful in handling this small amount, so now I will give you many more responsibilities.   *Matthew 25:21*

Much is required from those to whom much is given, and much more is required from those to whom much more is given.   *Luke 12:48*

Whatever you eat or drink or whatever you do, you must do all for the glory of God.   *1 Corinthians 10:31*

THE ABILITIES YOU HAVE are gifts from God, and with them comes the responsibility for using them well. You may have natural gifts in the areas of cooking, entertaining, managing a business, sewing, handling money, playing an instrument, or many other things. Use whatever gifts you have been given to bring honor and glory to God.

God's Promise

To those who use well what they are given, even more will be given, and they will have an abundance.
Matthew 25:29

A Servant Heart

*I need an attitude adjustment when it comes to
serving others. How can I see things differently?*

God's Response

Your attitude should be the same that Christ Jesus had.
Though he was God, he did not demand and cling to his
rights as God. . . . He obediently humbled himself . . . by
dying a criminal's death on a cross.   *Philippians 2:5-6, 8*

GOD GIVES EVERYONE specific abilities and strengths.
Sometimes we neglect to use those abilities, or we get
in the rut of using them only for ourselves (on a hobby,
for example). When we see our abilities as gifts from
almighty God, it is humbling to think that he would value
us enough to put these gifts within our care. Use them
for your personal enjoyment, but use them also to serve
others, for that is where they have the greatest impact.
We can pass on the gift of our abilities to others again
and again without running out. Through this act of serving others, we will find the attitude adjustment we seek.
Humble gratitude will pave the way.

God's Promise

God has given gifts to each of you from his great variety
of spiritual gifts. Manage them well so that God's
generosity can flow through you.   *1 Peter 4:10*

Heart Choice

How can I serve God today?

God's Response

Love the LORD your God, walk in all his ways, obey his commands, be faithful to him, and serve him with all your heart and all your soul.   *Joshua 22:5*

Choose today whom you will serve. . . . But as for me and my family, we will serve the LORD.   *Joshua 24:15*

E VERY DAY PRESENTS NEW CHOICES. The choice that you can always make—and only you can make it—is to honor God and obey his Word. This puts you squarely in the center of his will and makes you available to serve him. It is not complicated, but it is a challenge to put God ahead of everything else. Joshua urged the Israelites to worship and honor God alone and to steer clear of the gods of the people in their new land. Each day offers the choice to serve the Lord.

God's Promise

If you give up your life for me, you will find true life.
Matthew 16:25

Pure Heart

What kind of heart does God desire for me?

God's Response

Never before had there been a king like Josiah, who turned to the LORD with all his heart and soul and strength. *2 Kings 23:25*

I know, my God, that you examine our hearts and rejoice when you find integrity there. You know I have done all this with good motives, and I have watched your people offer their gifts willingly and joyously.   *1 Chronicles 29:17*

Teach me your ways, O LORD, that I may live according to your truth! Grant me purity of heart, that I may honor you.   *Psalm 86:11*

GOD DESIRES A TEACHABLE HEART of integrity, one that is pure, joyful, and devoted. This kind of heart honors and delights him. We will never fully achieve these qualities in this life, but God is pleased when we truly desire a heart like this. Do your best to move in that direction today.

God's Promise

God blesses those whose hearts are pure, for they will see God.   *Matthew 5:8*

All Your Heart

How can my heart become the heart God desires?

God's Response

Put all your rebellion behind you, and get for yourselves a new heart and a new spirit.   *Ezekiel 18:31*

I will give you a new heart with new and right desires, and I will put a new spirit in you. I will take out your stony heart of sin and give you a new, obedient heart.   *Ezekiel 36:26*

You must love the Lord your God with all your heart, all your soul, and all your mind.   *Matthew 22:37*

GOD WILL GIVE YOU A NEW HEART when you humble yourself before him, turn away from sinful habits, and make a daily effort to connect with him. When you do this, your love for him will grow. He can change even the coldest heart of stone into an obedient and loving heart. Are you willing to change?

God's Promise

Just think how much more the blood of Christ will purify our hearts from deeds that lead to death so that we can worship the living God.   *Hebrews 9:14*

　　　　　　　　　# Whole Heart

*Can I trust God enough to give him
my whole heart?*

God's Response

[God] never changes or casts shifting shadows. In his
goodness he chose to make us his own children by giving
us his true word.   *James 1:17-18*

God is not a man, that he should lie. . . . Has he ever
promised and not carried it through?   *Numbers 23:19*

WE TRUST ONLY THOSE WHO are dependable and can
be counted on to always tell the truth. As the creator, God is the source of truth, and therefore he cannot
lie. You must believe that in order to believe the following
statement: Because God cannot lie, everything he says in
the Bible is true. If it were not true, we could not fully
trust God. Keep reading your Bible. Find God's promises
to you. Discover how much he loves you and wants a
close, daily relationship with you. When you trust him
with your whole heart, he will make himself known to
you in amazing and powerful ways.

God's Promise

The Lord is faithful; he will make you strong and guard
you from the evil one.   *2 Thessalonians 3:3*

Heartbreak

How can I recover from a broken heart?

God's Response

From the ends of the earth, I will cry to you for help, for my heart is overwhelmed. Lead me to the towering rock of safety.   *Psalm 61:2*

Come quickly, LORD, and answer me, for my depression deepens. Don't turn away from me, or I will die. Let me hear of your unfailing love to me in the morning, for I am trusting you. Show me where to walk, for I have come to you in prayer.   *Psalm 143:7-8*

THERE IS NO QUICK ANTIDOTE for a broken heart. No pill, taken twice a day for two weeks, will cure it. A broken heart needs a different kind of healing—and doses of compassion, listening, love, comfort, encouragement, and blessing will eventually restore joy and hope to your soul. God is the master healer. Others can help, but no one can touch your broken heart and heal it as he can. When you are hurting, move toward God, not away from him. He is the greatest source of joy and healing.

God's Promise

He heals the brokenhearted, binding up their wounds. *Psalm 147:3*

Guard Your Heart

How can I guard and protect my heart?

God's Response

Above all else, guard your heart, for it affects everything you do.   *Proverbs 4:23*

Dear children, keep away from anything that might take God's place in your hearts.   *1 John 5:21*

My child, listen and be wise: Keep your heart on the right course.   *Proverbs 23:19*

PROTECT YOUR HEART FROM evil influences and temptations by obeying God and by staying away from anything that might tempt you to sin. This is very difficult in today's world. Renew your commitment to love God with all you have. This will help you to step toward him and not away from him when temptations come to call.

God's Challenge

You must always act in the fear of the LORD, with integrity and with undivided hearts.   *2 Chronicles 19:9*

Pursued by God

How much does God love me?

God's Response

For his unfailing love toward those who fear him is as great as the height of the heavens above the earth.   *Psalm 103:11*

Surely your goodness and unfailing love will pursue me all the days of my life, and I will live in the house of the LORD forever.   *Psalm 23:6*

Long ago the LORD said to Israel: "I have loved you, my people, with an everlasting love. With unfailing love I have drawn you to myself."   *Jeremiah 31:3*

GOD CREATED YOU, LOVES YOU, and longs to have a relationship with you. He pursues you and draws you to himself with persistent and unfailing love. Ask God to open your spiritual eyes today to see which events, conversations, chance meetings, thoughts, and open doors are God's hand reaching out to show you that he is nearby and at work in your life.

God's Promise

Do not be afraid or discouraged. For the LORD your God is with you wherever you go.   *Joshua 1:9*

Lost and Found

How does God show his love for me?

God's Response

I, the Son of Man, have come to seek and save those like him who are lost.   *Luke 19:10*

The law was given through Moses; God's unfailing love and faithfulness came through Jesus Christ.   *John 1:17*

When I am lifted up on the cross, I will draw everyone to myself.   *John 12:32*

YOU CAN KNOW THE DEPTH of Jesus' love because he died for you. God pursued you all the way to earth and took on our humanity so that he could draw you to himself for eternity. You once were lost, but Jesus found you—and he won't let you go.

God's Promise

God showed how much he loved us by sending his only Son into the world so that we might have eternal life through him.   *1 John 4:9*

With You Always

How can I know that Jesus is always with me?

God's Response

Be sure of this: I am with you always, even to the end of the age. *Matthew 28:20*

He is the Holy Spirit, who leads into all truth. The world at large cannot receive him, because it isn't looking for him and doesn't recognize him. But you do, because he lives with you now and later will be in you. *John 14:17*

I know the LORD is always with me. I will not be shaken, for he is right beside me. *Psalm 16:8*

JESUS PROMISED TO BE WITH his followers forever. That happens through the Holy Spirit, who lives in those who believe. Thus, you can never be alone when you believe in Jesus; he will not abandon those he has created in love.

God's Promise

Do not be afraid, for I am with you. *Isaiah 43:5*

God's Desire for You

Why does God desire me?

God's Response

He loves us with unfailing love; the faithfulness of the LORD endures forever. Praise the LORD!   *Psalm 117:2*

You are a God of forgiveness, gracious and merciful, slow to become angry, and full of unfailing love and mercy. *Nehemiah 9:17*

See how very much our heavenly Father loves us, for he allows us to be called his children.   *1 John 3:1*

My heart has heard you say, "Come and talk with me." And my heart responds, "LORD, I am coming."   *Psalm 27:8*

GOD LOVES YOU BECAUSE HE MADE YOU. You are not a random creature evolved from a prehistoric primordial soup. God created you in his own image to have a relationship with him. God desires your friendship, and he is courting you now. Pursue him and discover the purpose for which you were made.

God's Promise

God loves you dearly, and he has called you to be his very own people.   *Romans 1:7*

Real Love

How can I know that God really loves me?

God's Response

God so loved the world that he gave his only Son, so that everyone who believes in him will not perish but have eternal life. *John 3:16*

This is real love. It is not that we loved God, but that he loved us and sent his Son as a sacrifice to take away our sins. *1 John 4:10*

Can anything ever separate us from Christ's love? *Romans 8:35*

YOU CAN KNOW FOR CERTAIN of God's great love for you because he allowed his Son to die in your place, to take the punishment for your sin so that you could be free from eternal judgment. Think of it: He sent his Son to die for you so that you could live forever with him. No wonder John wrote, "This is real love."

God's Promise

I will never fail you. I will never forsake you. *Hebrews 13:5*

Responding to God's Love

How can I show my love for God?

God's Response

If you love me, obey my commandments.   *John 14:15*

When you obey me, you remain in my love. . . . I have told you this so that you will be filled with my joy. Yes, your joy will overflow!   *John 15:10-11*

No, O people, the LORD has already told you what is good, and this is what he requires: to do what is right, to love mercy, and to walk humbly with your God.   *Micah 6:8*

OBEDIENCE EXPRESSES YOUR love for God. This should not be confused with earning God's love by doing good works. You obey God because you are already loved, not in order to be loved. As you obey, you will experience increasing joy because you will see God at work in your life every day. What small step of obedience can you take right now?

God's Promise

If you will obey me and keep my covenant, you will be my own special treasure from among all the nations of the earth; for all the earth belongs to me.   *Exodus 19:5*

Intimacy
with God

What does it mean to be intimate with God?

God's Response

I will be with you, and I will protect you wherever you go. . . . I will be with you constantly until I have finished giving you everything I have promised.   *Genesis 28:15*

"In that coming day," says the LORD, "you will call me 'my husband' instead of 'my master.' . . . I will make you my wife forever, showing you righteousness and justice, unfailing love and compassion."   *Hosea 2:16, 19*

THE WORDS *GOD IS LOVE* MEAN that God is the source of love, the only One who could create us with the ability to love. Therefore, no one knows as much about love as God does. Intimacy with God means experiencing his love to the fullest and returning that love to him. The love he communicates is completely loyal, trusting, serving, and revealing. God created marriage, for example, to illustrate what an intimate relationship with him should look like.

God's Promise

The LORD your God has arrived to live among you. . . . He will exult over you by singing a happy song.
Zephaniah 3:17

Always There

What does intimacy with God mean for me today?

God's Response

The LORD replied, "I will personally go with you."
Exodus 33:14

The LORD is my shepherd; I have everything I need. He lets me rest in green meadows; he leads me beside peaceful streams. . . . Even when I walk through the dark valley of death, I will not be afraid, for you are close beside me. Your rod and your staff protect and comfort me.
Psalm 23:1-2, 4

INTIMACY WITH GOD PROVIDES a close relationship that helps you see his personal touch on your life every day. He is your shepherd and creator. He wants to communicate with you, watch out for you, care for you, advise you, and give you his joy and blessings. You must work with him as he guides you, step-by-step. When you stay close to him, you will see him act on your behalf. Look for him in your life today, and you will notice him.

God's Promise

Surely your goodness and unfailing love will pursue me all the days of my life, and I will live in the house of the LORD forever.   *Psalm 23:6*

Draw Close

What must I do to experience intimacy with God?

God's Response

My heart has heard you say, "Come and talk with me." And my heart responds, "LORD, I am coming."   *Psalm 27:8*

The LORD is close to all who call on him, yes, to all who call on him sincerely.   *Psalm 145:18*

Draw close to God, and God will draw close to you. *James 4:8*

IF YOU WANT INTIMACY WITH GOD, you need to draw close to him, talk to him, respond to him, and call on him sincerely. If you have a dear friend, you do your best to stay in touch. It's no different with God. He promises that as you draw close to him, he will draw close to you.

God's Promise

If you seek him, you will find him.   *1 Chronicles 28:9*

Holy before Him

With all my faults, how can I have intimacy with God?

God's Response

We can boldly enter heaven's Most Holy Place because of the blood of Jesus. This is the new, life-giving way that Christ has opened up for us through the sacred curtain, by means of his death for us. And since we have a great High Priest who rules over God's people, let us go right into the presence of God, with true hearts fully trusting him. For our evil consciences have been sprinkled with Christ's blood to make us clean, and our bodies have been washed with pure water.   *Hebrews 10:19-22*

BECAUSE OF JESUS CHRIST'S life, death, and resurrection—and your faith in him—you stand holy and blameless in God's presence. You can come to him confidently. Jesus died for you—why would he turn you away?

God's Promise

He has brought you back as his friends. He has done this through his death on the cross in his own human body. As a result, he has brought you into the very presence of God, and you are holy and blameless as you stand before him without a single fault.   *Colossians 1:22*

God's Presence

How can I enter God's presence?

God's Response

From there you will search again for the LORD your God. And if you search for him with all your heart and soul, you will find him.   *Deuteronomy 4:29*

Let us come boldly to the throne of our gracious God. There we will receive his mercy, and we will find grace to help us when we need it.   *Hebrews 4:16*

GOD IS WITH YOU AT ALL TIMES, everywhere, and you can draw near to him anytime and anyplace. Go boldly, knowing that a loving and gracious God awaits you with grace and mercy.

God's Promise

Look! Here I stand at the door and knock. If you hear me calling and open the door, I will come in, and we will share a meal as friends.   *Revelation 3:20*

God with You

What are some benefits of having God with me?

God's Response

You will show me the way of life, granting me the joy of your presence and the pleasures of living with you forever. *Psalm 16:11*

I command you—be strong and courageous! Do not be afraid or discouraged. For the LORD your God is with you wherever you go. *Joshua 1:9*

WHEN GOD IS WITH YOU, you experience more freedom from sin and its consequences, more joy because you are in the center of his will, and more courage to face whatever life brings your way. Your all-powerful God is close by.

God's Promise

When you go through deep waters and great trouble, I will be with you. When you go through rivers of difficulty, you will not drown! When you walk through the fire of oppression, you will not be burned up; the flames will not consume you. *Isaiah 43:2*

God's Nearness

What should I do when God seems far away?

God's Response

I can never escape from your spirit! I can never get away from your presence! . . . If I ride the wings of the morning, if I dwell by the farthest oceans, even there your hand will guide me, and your strength will support me. *Psalm 139:7, 9-10*

Can a mother forget her nursing child? Can she feel no love for a child she has borne? But even if that were possible, I would not forget you! *Isaiah 49:15*

WHEN GOD SEEMS FAR AWAY, it is because we have moved away from him, not because he has moved away from us. Return to him in prayer, in humility, and in faith. He is waiting for you.

God's Promise

I will make an everlasting covenant with them, promising not to stop doing good for them. I will put a desire in their hearts to worship me, and they will never leave me. *Jeremiah 32:40*

God's Presence

Is God absent in my times of pain and trouble?

God's Response

When the traders came by, his brothers pulled Joseph out of the pit and sold him for twenty pieces of silver. . . . The LORD was with Joseph, giving him success in everything he did.   *Genesis 37:28; 39:3*

We are hunted down, but God never abandons us. We get knocked down, but we get up again and keep going. *2 Corinthians 4:9*

GOD WILL NEVER DESERT those who follow him. He doesn't take the day off and forget about you. When you accidentally cut yourself, you become completely focused on how bad it is and on how to stop the bleeding. In the same way, our problems and troubles can focus us so much on getting rid of the pain that we neglect God, forgetting that he has promised to help us in our difficulties. To abandon you, God would have to cease loving you, and he cannot do that, for he is love.

God's Promise

The LORD will not abandon his chosen people. *1 Samuel 12:22*

Suffering

Does suffering mean that God doesn't care about me?

God's Response

He has not ignored the suffering of the needy. He has not turned and walked away. He has listened to their cries for help.   *Psalm 22:24*

You keep track of all my sorrows. You have collected all my tears in your bottle. You have recorded each one in your book.   *Psalm 56:8*

S UFFERING IS NOT A SIGN THAT God doesn't care. It is simply a fact of life in this fallen world. God promises to be with you in the midst of whatever you are struggling with. He may not remove the difficulty from you, but he does promise to help you get through it. Your suffering matters to God because you matter to God. God cares so much that not a single tear goes unnoticed.

God's Promise

Those who plant in tears will harvest with shouts of joy. They weep as they go to plant their seed, but they sing as they return with the harvest.   *Psalm 126:5-6*

Distress

How do I talk to God when I am in trouble?

God's Response

In my distress I cried out to the LORD; yes, I prayed to my God for help. He heard me from his sanctuary; my cry reached his ears.   *Psalm 18:6*

The LORD hears his people when they call to him for help. *Psalm 34:17*

GOD HEARS EVERY PRAYER that you think or say. He also responds—not always in the way that you want him to, but always in a way that will make you stronger and wiser. A muscle grows only when it works against a greater weight. Your character will grow as it struggles with things that seem too much for you. When you are in distress, ask God to help you learn from the experience. Make the most of the opportunity to give the muscles of your character enough exercise.

God's Promise

When they call on me, I will answer; I will be with them in trouble. I will rescue them and honor them. *Psalm 91:15*

Good from Bad

Can any good come from my suffering?

God's Response

Consider the joy of those corrected by God! Do not despise the chastening of the Almighty when you sin. For though he wounds, he also bandages. *Job 5:17-18*

Since I know it is all for Christ's good, I am quite content with my weaknesses and with insults, hardships, persecutions, and calamities. For when I am weak, then I am strong. *2 Corinthians 12:10*

S OMETIMES YOU MAY SUFFER because you are dealing with the consequences of sin. At other times, suffering occurs from hardships outside your control. At all times when your faith is tested, you have the opportunity to learn and grow, so take advantage of that opportunity. It will help you to deal better with suffering in the future, and it will teach you to recognize and avoid certain troubles down the road.

God's Promise

We can rejoice, too, when we run into problems and trials, for we know that they are good for us—they help us learn to endure. And endurance develops strength of character. *Romans 5:3-4*

Past Sins

If I know I'm suffering because of past sins, will God still forgive me?

God's Response

I assure you that any sin can be forgiven.   *Mark 3:28*

He forgives all my sins and heals all my diseases. . . . He has not punished us for all our sins, nor does he deal with us as we deserve.   *Psalm 103:3, 10*

If we say we have no sin, we are only fooling ourselves and refusing to accept the truth. But if we confess our sins to him, he is faithful and just to forgive us and to cleanse us from every wrong.   *1 John 1:8-9*

FORGIVENESS MEANS THAT God looks at you as though you had never sinned. When he forgives you, you are blameless before him. God doesn't sweep your sins under the carpet; instead, he completely washes them away. If you have confessed your sin, don't go through another day under the weight of unnecessary guilt.

God's Promise

I—yes, I alone—am the one who blots out your sins for my own sake and will never think of them again. *Isaiah 43:25*

Confession

What happens when I confess my sin?

God's Response

Please pardon the sins of this people because of your magnificent, unfailing love.   *Numbers 14:19*

There is no condemnation for those who belong to Christ Jesus.   *Romans 8:1*

Everyone who believes in him will have their sins forgiven through his name.   *Acts 10:43*

CONFESSION IS THE ACT of recognizing our sins before God so he can forgive us. Sin separates us from a holy God; confession indicates our desire to be in a right relationship with him. When you confess your sin, you agree that something wrong needs to be made right and that a damaged relationship needs to be restored.

God's Promise

This is my blood, which seals the covenant between God and his people. It is poured out to forgive the sins of many.   *Matthew 26:28*

Forgiving Others

How does God's forgiveness help me to forgive others?

God's Response

If you forgive those who sin against you, your heavenly Father will forgive you. But if you refuse to forgive others, your Father will not forgive your sins.   *Matthew 6:14-15*

Peter came to him and asked, "Lord, how often should I forgive someone who sins against me? Seven times?"
    "No!" Jesus replied, "seventy times seven!"
Matthew 18:21-22

GOD'S FORGIVENESS SAVES US from hell and gives us a ticket to heaven, where sin and suffering will be gone forever. This is the greatest gift any person can receive, and yet no person deserves it. Any forgiveness you extend to someone else pales in comparison to the forgiveness God has extended to you. Refusing to forgive shows that you have not understood the cost or the power of God's forgiveness. Just as God forgives you without limit, you should forgive others without keeping count.

God's Challenge

You must make allowance for each other's faults and forgive the person who offends you. Remember, the Lord forgave you, so you must forgive others.   *Colossians 3:13*

Unlimited Forgiveness

Is there a limit to how much God will forgive me?

God's Response

All their past sins will be forgotten, and they will live because of the righteous things they have done.   *Ezekiel 18:22*

With my authority, take this message of repentance to all the nations, beginning in Jerusalem: "There is forgiveness of sins for all who turn to me."   *Luke 24:47*

He is so rich in kindness that he purchased our freedom through the blood of his Son, and our sins are forgiven. *Ephesians 1:7*

NO MATTER HOW GREAT YOUR SIN or how many times you have sinned, God will forgive you if you are sincerely sorry for what you have done and confess your sin to him. This is called repentance. To think that some of your sins are "too big" to be forgiven is to think too little of Jesus' sacrifice on your behalf.

God's Promise

God has purchased our freedom with his blood and has forgiven all our sins.   *Colossians 1:14*

Mood Swings

My emotions go up and down.
How can I best handle them?

God's Response

Many of the older priests, Levites, and other leaders remembered the first Temple, and they wept aloud when they saw the new Temple's foundation. The others, however, were shouting for joy. The joyful shouting and weeping mingled together in a loud commotion that could be heard far in the distance.   *Ezra 3:12-13*

GOD CREATED YOUR EMOTIONS, and it's perfectly natural to experience highs and lows. However, your emotions can distract you from God if you worry too much, get caught up in doing the wrong things, or let anger control you. Don't deny your emotions, but don't let them master you or cause you to sin. God has given you the emotions of sorrow and joy, peace and anguish, love and anger, gratitude and doubt, and all can be used to deepen your relationship with him. Express all your feelings to him and let him address your needs.

God's Promise

Knowing God leads to self-control. Self-control leads to patient endurance, and patient endurance leads to godliness.   *2 Peter 1:6*

Depression

Does God care when I feel depressed?

God's Response

He was despised and rejected—a man of sorrows, acquainted with bitterest grief.   *Isaiah 53:3*

He heals the brokenhearted, binding up their wounds. *Psalm 147:3*

God blesses those who mourn, for they will be comforted. *Matthew 5:4*

JESUS SUFFERED AS DEEPLY as any human could; he was acquainted with bitter grief. Because he can relate to your pain, and because of his great love for you, God understands and cares when you are hurting. His heart breaks along with yours. He is with you in your pain, and he promises to bless you in the midst of it. Look for that extra measure of comfort from him today.

God's Promise

The LORD is close to the brokenhearted; he rescues those who are crushed in spirit.   *Psalm 34:18*

God's Touch

What can I do when I am depressed?
How can I recover?

God's Response

[Elijah] went on alone into the desert, traveling all day. He sat down under a solitary broom tree and prayed that he might die. "I have had enough, LORD," he said. . . . Then he lay down and slept under the broom tree. But as he was sleeping, an angel touched him and told him, "Get up and eat!" He looked around and saw some bread baked on hot stones and a jar of water! So he ate and drank and lay down again.   *1 Kings 19:4-6*

RECOVERY FROM DEPRESSION involves a number of factors, including a new perspective. Elijah was tired, hungry, and feeling completely alone. A period of rest, good food, and reengagement with God helped him to regain a proper perspective and to reconnect with God's purpose for his life. We can become depressed when we've lost the larger perspective of what God wants us to do. If you're feeling depressed, begin with rest, good nutrition, and reengagement with God. If you still need help, a godly counselor can help you regain a right perspective.

God's Promise

Your Father already knows your needs.   *Luke 12:30*

God's Voice

How will God speak to me in my depression?

God's Response

"Go out and stand before me on the mountain," the LORD told him. And as Elijah stood there, the LORD passed by, and a mighty windstorm hit the mountain. It was such a terrible blast that the rocks were torn loose, but the LORD was not in the wind. After the wind there was an earthquake, but the LORD was not in the earthquake. And after the earthquake there was a fire, but the LORD was not in the fire. And after the fire there was the sound of a gentle whisper.   *1 Kings 19:11-12*

YOU MAY WISH THAT GOD would break through the darkness with a mighty blast and make the sadness simply disappear. Don't expect that from God, although it may happen that way. Instead, listen for his Spirit's gentle whisper in the quietness of your heart. He will speak to you. Seek a quiet place in which to hear him.

God's Promise

LORD, you know the hopes of the helpless. Surely you will listen to their cries and comfort them.   *Psalm 10:17*

Discouragement

I'm feeling a bit discouraged.
What can I do about that?

God's Response

Why am I discouraged? Why so sad? I will put my hope in God! I will praise him again—my Savior and my God! Now I am deeply discouraged, but I will remember your kindness. . . . Through each day the LORD pours his unfailing love upon me, and through each night I sing his songs, praying to God who gives me life.   *Psalm 42:5-6, 8*

WITH EVERYTHING THAT CAN GO wrong in life, and with all there is to do, it is easy to become discouraged. In fact, discouragement is one of the most common emotions. Encouragement is the best antidote to discouragement. Read the verses above once more. God is your greatest encourager. Allow him to encourage you each day through his Word. This will lead you to encourage others, and some will return to you in gratitude, further encouraging you. If God has encouraged you, is there someone you can encourage today?

God's Promise

God . . . encourages those who are discouraged.
2 Corinthians 7:6

Focusing on God

How can I resist feelings of discouragement?

God's Response

Don't be troubled. You trust God, now trust in me.
John 14:1

Don't get tired of doing what is good. Don't get discouraged and give up, for we will reap a harvest of blessing at the appropriate time.   *Galatians 6:9*

WHEN YOU FEEL DISCOURAGED, it is easy to turn inward and become paralyzed by your own feelings and pain. It takes great effort, but refocus your attention on God. Every day he opens doors of opportunity that can bring purpose and meaning to you: helping someone in need, giving time to a good cause, writing a note of encouragement. When you lift your eyes from the ground, you will see the door God has opened. Walk through it with courage, and on the other side you will find great encouragement.

God's Promise

This is what the LORD Almighty says: All this may seem impossible to you now, a small and discouraged remnant of God's people. But do you think this is impossible for me, the LORD Almighty?   *Zechariah 8:6*

Staying Strong

How can I help a friend who is feeling discouraged?

God's Response

"He may have a great army, but they are just men. We have the LORD our God to help us and to fight our battles for us!" These words greatly encouraged the people. *2 Chronicles 32:8*

When others are happy, be happy with them. If they are sad, share their sorrow.   *Romans 12:15*

Jonathan went to find David and encouraged him to stay strong in his faith in God.   *1 Samuel 23:16*

I F A FRIEND IS DISCOURAGED, be kind and empathetic. Sometimes just being there is all that is needed. Ask the Lord for wisdom. You may be able to encourage her to stay close to God, reminding her that God is with her in her troubles.

God's Promise

Do not be afraid or discouraged, for the LORD is the one who goes before you. He will be with you; he will neither fail you nor forsake you.   *Deuteronomy 31:8*

Building Others Up

How can I build others up and offer encouragement?

God's Response

Judge fairly and honestly, and show mercy and kindness to one another.   *Zechariah 7:9*

All of you should be of one mind, full of sympathy toward each other, loving one another with tender hearts and humble minds.   *1 Peter 3:8*

Be humble and gentle. Be patient with each other, making allowance for each other's faults because of your love. *Ephesians 4:2*

YOU BUILD OTHERS UP BY FINDING what is good in them and complimenting them. Don't flatter people just to make them feel good; that isn't honest. But a small word of honest encouragement can often make someone's day. If you have a reputation for integrity, others will know that your words are true.

God's Promise

Dear brothers and sisters, I close my letter with these last words: Rejoice. Change your ways. Encourage each other. Live in harmony and peace. Then the God of love and peace will be with you.   *2 Corinthians 13:11*

Compliments

Why is it important to compliment others?

God's Response

Every time I think of you, I give thanks to my God. I always pray for you, and I make my requests with a heart full of joy. *Philippians 1:3-4*

Dear brothers and sisters, we always thank God for you, as is right, for we are thankful that your faith is flourishing and you are all growing in love for each other. *2 Thessalonians 1:3*

PAUL THOUGHT IT WAS very important to compliment the believers in the various churches on the spiritual growth he saw in them. The way his love for them overflows in his words is a model for us. You can do the same, encouraging others about their spiritual growth or about any other aspect of their lives. Criticism tears others down; compliments build them up. Who couldn't use an uplifting compliment?

God's Promise

Worry weighs a person down; an encouraging word cheers a person up. *Proverbs 12:25*

True Words

How do I know if I'm giving a true compliment and not flattery?

God's Response

Even when you do ask, you don't get it because your whole motive is wrong—you want only what will give you pleasure. *James 4:3*

May the words of my mouth and the thoughts of my heart be pleasing to you, O LORD, my rock and my redeemer. *Psalm 19:14*

In the end, people appreciate frankness more than flattery. *Proverbs 28:23*

THE DIFFERENCE BETWEEN a compliment and flattery is found in the motivation behind the words. A sincere compliment is about the other person, designed to build him or her up. Flattery is all about you, saying something nice just to get something in return. Never ignore your conscience—it will tell you if you are being sincere.

God's Promise

He died for us so that we can live with him forever. . . . So encourage each other and build each other up, just as you are already doing. *1 Thessalonians 5:10-11*

He Cares

How does God show he cares for me?

God's Response

Yes, you have been with me from birth; from my mother's womb you have cared for me. No wonder I am always praising you!   *Psalm 71:6*

If God cares so wonderfully for flowers that are here today and gone tomorrow, won't he more surely care for you? You have so little faith!   *Matthew 6:30*

G OD CARES FOR YOU because he made you. He knew your name before you were born. When you doubt this, you stop looking for his care and miss the doors of opportunity and blessing he has opened wide for you. Look at your life differently today. Watch for signs of his love and care. Don't assume that the good things coming into your life are coincidental. Realize that they express God's loving care for you. Start trusting him to show you this same care during hard times.

God's Promise

I will be your God throughout your lifetime—until your hair is white with age. I made you, and I will care for you. I will carry you along and save you.
Isaiah 46:4

How can I show others that I care about them?

God's Response

I was naked, and you gave me clothing. I was sick, and you cared for me. I was in prison, and you visited me. *Matthew 25:36*

The Samaritan soothed his wounds with medicine. . . . Then he . . . took him to an inn, where he took care of him.   *Luke 10:34*

If you give even a cup of cold water to one of the least of my followers, you will surely be rewarded.   *Matthew 10:42*

ARE YOU AN ALL-OR-NOTHING BELIEVER? Too often we think that if we are not doing something big for God, we might as well do nothing. Don't confuse *big* with *significant*. A simple act of kindness (a phone call, a note, making dinner for a shut-in, watching babies in the nursery) is not big in the world's eyes, but it is significant to God. Even giving a cup of cold water brings God's approval.

God's Challenge

Pure and lasting religion in the sight of God our Father means that we must care for orphans and widows in their troubles, and refuse to let the world corrupt us. *James 1:27*

Eagles' Wings

I'm worn out. Should I give up or keep going?

God's Response

Don't you know that the LORD is the everlasting God, the Creator of all the earth? He never grows faint or weary. . . . He gives power to those who are tired and worn out; he offers strength to the weak. Even youths will become exhausted, and young men will give up. But those who wait on the LORD will find new strength. They will fly high on wings like eagles. They will run and not grow weary. They will walk and not faint. *Isaiah 40:28-31*

B EING BONE WEARY IS DANGEROUS because it can keep you from thinking clearly and cause you to do or say something you'll regret. You must recognize your human limitations. Learn when to say no so that you aren't tapped out for those to whom you need to say yes. Then, like the eagle that depends on the wind currents to keep it soaring, you can count on the supernatural Spirit of the Lord to lift you up and keep you doing what he has called you to do.

God's Promise

This light and power that now shine within us . . . [are] held in perishable containers, that is, in our weak bodies. So everyone can see that our glorious power is from God and is not our own. *2 Corinthians 4:7*

Energy

How can I find more energy?

God's Response

Six days a week are set apart for your daily duties and regular work, but the seventh day is a day of rest.   *Exodus 20:9-10*

Jesus said, "Let's get away from the crowds for a while and rest." There were so many people coming and going that Jesus and his apostles didn't even have time to eat. *Mark 6:31*

It is useless for you to work so hard from early morning until late at night, anxiously working for food to eat; for God gives rest to his loved ones.   *Psalm 127:2*

REST IS NOT A SUGGESTION FROM GOD; it is a commandment. Most of us don't get enough of it. Rest is not just sleeping; it is doing something different from your normal work, something that will refresh and reward you. Since God modeled rest for us, there is no doubt but that we will find spiritual significance in it.

God's Promise

I have given rest to the weary.   *Jeremiah 31:25*

Energy

Will God supply me with more energy?

God's Response

It is not by force nor by strength, but by my Spirit, says the Lord Almighty.   *Zechariah 4:6*

I pray that from his glorious, unlimited resources he will give you mighty inner strength through his Holy Spirit. *Ephesians 3:16*

I say to the rest of you, dear brothers and sisters, never get tired of doing good.   *2 Thessalonians 3:13*

THE HOLY SPIRIT IS THE POWER of God that lives in the believer. When you yield control of your life to the Lord, he releases his power within you—power to resist temptation, to serve and love God and others when you are at the end of your rope, to have wisdom in all circumstances, and to persevere in living for God now with the promise of eternal life later. Through his Spirit, God will give you the energy you need to do all that he asks you to do.

God's Promise

I can do everything with the help of Christ who gives me the strength I need.   *Philippians 4:13*

Praise

The Lord has helped me in so many ways.
How can I thank him?

God's Response

Praise the LORD! I will thank the LORD with all my heart. . . . How amazing are the deeds of the LORD! All who delight in him should ponder them.   *Psalm 111:1-2*

With all my heart I will praise you, O LORD my God. I will give glory to your name forever.   *Psalm 86:12*

Who can list the glorious miracles of the LORD? Who can ever praise him half enough?   *Psalm 106:2*

YOU CAN EXPRESS YOUR THANKS through praise. Thankfulness goes beyond gratitude for something; it also acknowledges the One from whom your blessings come. When you thank God for answered prayer and for his work in your life, you are acknowledging his help and worshiping him for who he is and what he does.

God's Challenge

Bring your petitions, and return to the LORD. Say to him, "Forgive all our sins and graciously receive us, so that we may offer you the sacrifice of praise."
Hosea 14:2

Perspective

How can I praise God when life is difficult?

God's Response

Joseph told them, " . . . God turned into good what you meant for evil." *Genesis 50:19-20*

No matter what happens, always be thankful, for this is God's will for you who belong to Christ Jesus. *1 Thessalonians 5:18*

L IFE CAN BE DIFFICULT FOR any number of reasons. You may experience the consequences of your own sin; you may suffer because of someone else's sin; you may be caught in circumstances that are no one's fault. God may be testing your faith, or you may be a target for Satan, who wants to disrupt your godly influence and discourage you. In any of these tough circumstances there is reason to praise God. He redeems our mistakes, teaches us wisdom through adversity, promises to help us through tough times, and guarantees eternal life free from suffering for all who are his followers. A God who redeems all trouble is a God worthy of praise.

God's Promise

He will remove all of their sorrows, and there will be no more death or sorrow or crying or pain. For the old world and its evils are gone forever. *Revelation 21:4*

Sure-Footedness

How should I respond to life's troubling circumstances?

God's Response

Even though the fig trees have no blossoms, and there are no grapes on the vine; even though the olive crop fails, and the fields lie empty and barren; even though the flocks die in the fields, and the cattle barns are empty, yet I will rejoice in the LORD! I will be joyful in the God of my salvation. The Sovereign LORD is my strength! He will make me as surefooted as a deer and bring me safely over the mountains. *Habakkuk 3:17-19*

A SPIRIT OF GRATITUDE AND PRAISE changes the way you look at life. Complaining connects you to your unhappiness—gratitude and praise connect you to the source of real joy. When you make thanksgiving a regular part of your life, you stay focused on all God has done and continues to do for you. Expressing gratitude for God's help is a form of worship.

God's Promise

Dear brothers and sisters, whenever trouble comes your way, let it be an opportunity for joy. For when your faith is tested, your endurance has a chance to grow. *James 1:2-3*

Such a Time as This

How can I make the most of my circumstances?

God's Response

Blessed are those who trust in the LORD and have made the LORD their hope and confidence. They are like trees planted along a riverbank, with roots that reach deep into the water. *Jeremiah 17:7-8*

Who can say but that you have been elevated to the palace for just such a time as this? *Esther 4:14*

GOD WANTS TO USE YOU RIGHT where you are. His guidance isn't just for your next big decision—he had a purpose in placing you where you are this moment. Look at your current circumstances as a calling from God. Serve and obey him in the little things today. God has placed you here for "such a time as this."

God's Promise

When darkness overtakes the godly, light will come bursting in. . . . Such people will not be overcome by evil circumstances. . . . They do not fear bad news; they confidently trust the LORD to care for them. They are confident and fearless and can face their foes triumphantly. *Psalm 112:4, 6-8*

Contentment

How can I find contentment regardless of life's circumstances?

God's Response

O God, you are my God; I earnestly search for you. My soul thirsts for you. . . . You satisfy me more than the richest of foods.   *Psalm 63:1, 5*

How wonderful it is, how pleasant, when brothers live together in harmony!   *Psalm 133:1*

God blesses those who realize their need for him, for the Kingdom of Heaven is given to them.   *Matthew 5:3*

THE BIBLE REPEATEDLY TEACHES that our deepest contentment and joy come not from the pursuit of happiness, pleasure, or material wealth but in the pursuit of an intimate relationship with God. You can serve God by serving others with his love. The harder you focus on pleasing yourself, the more you will miss it. The more you take the focus off yourself, the more content you will be.

God's Promise

You will keep in perfect peace all who trust in you, whose thoughts are fixed on you!   *Isaiah 26:3*

Staying Power

How can I develop perseverance through
my circumstances?

God's Response

I think you ought to know, dear brothers and sisters, about the trouble we went through in the province of Asia. We were crushed and completely overwhelmed, and we thought we would never live through it. In fact, we expected to die. But as a result, we learned not to rely on ourselves, but on God who can raise the dead.   *2 Corinthians 1:8-9*

I am sure that God, who began the good work within you, will continue his work until it is finally finished on that day when Christ Jesus comes back again.   *Philippians 1:6*

THE KEY TO PERSEVERANCE is having a clear view of heaven as your destination. When you see clearly where you are going, it is easier to endure the hardships along the road. God promises to help you. His persistent and faithful work in your life gives you the supernatural power to keep going when you encounter difficulties.

God's Promise

May the Lord bring you into an ever deeper understanding of the love of God and the endurance that comes from Christ.   *2 Thessalonians 3:5*

Overwhelming Worry

Where can I turn when worry overwhelms me?

God's Response

I tell you, don't worry about everyday life—whether you have enough food, drink, and clothes. Doesn't life consist of more than food and clothing? Look at the birds. They don't need to plant or harvest or put food in barns because your heavenly Father feeds them. And you are far more valuable to him than they are. Can all your worries add a single moment to your life? Of course not. . . . Your heavenly Father already knows all your needs, and he will give you all you need from day to day if you live for him and make the Kingdom of God your primary concern.   *Matthew 6:25-27, 32-33*

JESUS' WORDS SUGGEST THREE QUESTIONS you can ask yourself when you start to worry about something: (1) Is it important? Many of our anxieties revolve around issues that are even less important than food and clothing. (2) Is it helpful? Worrying is useless; in fact, it's usually counter-productive. (3) Who is in charge? God is in control, and your heavenly Father delights to meet your needs. As you ask and answer these questions, your anxiety will diminish.

God's Promise

Give your burdens to the LORD, and he will take care of you.   *Psalm 55:22*

Gracious Provision

Does God really care about my daily needs?

God's Response

This same God who takes care of me will supply all your needs from his glorious riches, which have been given to us in Christ Jesus. *Philippians 4:19*

God will generously provide all you need. Then you will always have everything you need and plenty left over to share with others. *2 Corinthians 9:8*

WE MUST LEARN TO DISTINGUISH between wants and needs. When we understand what we truly need and see how God provides, we will realize how much he truly cares for us. God doesn't promise to give you a lot of possessions, but he does promise to help you possess the character traits that reflect his nature so that you can accomplish his plan for you. He doesn't promise to preserve your physical life, but he does promise to keep your soul for all eternity if you've pledged your allegiance to him.

God's Promise

I will be your God throughout your lifetime—until your hair is white with age. I made you, and I will care for you. *Isaiah 46:4*

Contentment

How can I keep a clear distinction between my needs and my wants?

God's Response

If we have enough food and clothing, let us be content. *1 Timothy 6:8*

First, help me never to tell a lie. Second, give me neither poverty nor riches! Give me just enough to satisfy my needs. *Proverbs 30:8*

Your Father knows exactly what you need even before you ask him! *Matthew 6:8*

YOU WILL NEVER BE CONTENT IF you focus on your wants, because you will always want more. That is why the Lord promises to supply your needs, not your wants. The more you focus on what the Lord values, the more you will be able to distinguish your needs from your wants. If you constantly feel discontented, you may be focusing more on what you want than on what God wants for you.

God's Promise

Let the LORD's people show him reverence, for those who honor him will have all they need. *Psalm 34:9*

Sharing What You Have

Why does God promise to meet my needs?

God's Response

One day a man from Baal-shalishah brought the man of God [Elisha] a sack of fresh grain and twenty loaves of barley bread made from the first grain of his harvest. Elisha said, "Give it to the group of prophets so they can eat."

"What?" his servant exclaimed. "Feed one hundred people with only this?"

But Elisha repeated, "Give it to the group of prophets so they can eat, for the LORD says there will be plenty for all. There will even be some left over!" And sure enough, there was plenty for all and some left over, just as the LORD had promised.   *2 Kings 4:42-44*

G OD GIVES TO YOU SO THAT YOU WILL be satisfied and so that you can give to others. Whether you have been richly blessed or have just enough to get by, the Lord promises that you will always have enough to share.

God's Promise

Don't forget to do good and to share what you have with those in need, for such sacrifices are very pleasing to God. *Hebrews 13:16*

Your Needs Supplied

What types of things does God promise to supply?

God's Response

When I pray, you answer me; you encourage me by giving me the strength I need.   *Psalm 138:3*

One day the apostles said to the Lord, "We need more faith; tell us how to get it."   *Luke 17:5*

Reverence for the LORD is the foundation of true wisdom. The rewards of wisdom come to all who obey him. Praise his name forever!   *Psalm 111:10*

God is faithful. He will keep the temptation from becoming so strong that you can't stand up against it. When you are tempted, he will show you a way out so that you will not give in to it.   *1 Corinthians 10:13*

GOD PROMISES ALWAYS TO meet certain needs. He will always meet your need for salvation, mercy, wisdom, comfort, strength, faith, and a way out of temptation. He does this through the Holy Spirit.

God's Promise

Since God did not spare even his own Son but gave him up for us all, won't God, who gave us Christ, also give us everything else?   *Romans 8:32*

Passing It On

God has shown such compassion for me.
How can I pass that along to others?

God's Response

You must be compassionate, just as your Father is compassionate.   *Luke 6:36*

The LORD is kind and merciful, slow to get angry, full of unfailing love.   *Psalm 145:8*

He will rescue the poor when they cry to him; he will help the oppressed, who have no one to defend them. He feels pity for the weak and the needy. . . . Their lives are precious to him.   *Psalm 72:12-14*

A **COMPASSIONATE HEART IS** a mark of godliness. Compassion spurs you to put your love into action and motivates you to meet the needs of others. You can pass along the compassion of Jesus by your willingness to care for others. What one act of compassion could you offer today?

God's Challenge

Be kind to each other, tenderhearted, forgiving one another, just as God through Christ has forgiven you.
Ephesians 4:32

Loving Your Neighbors

How am I to love my neighbors?

God's Response

Always judge your neighbors fairly, neither favoring the poor nor showing deference to the rich. Do not spread slanderous gossip among your people. Do not try to get ahead at the cost of your neighbor's life, for I am the LORD.   *Leviticus 19:15-16*

Love your neighbor as yourself.   *Matthew 22:39*

WHY DID JESUS SAY TO love your neighbor as yourself? Because God knows that our first instinct is to take care of ourselves. If we can train ourselves to think of others as being just as important to us as we are, then we have truly made them a priority. And caring for others is what love is all about.

God's Promise

It is good when you truly obey our Lord's royal command found in the Scriptures: "Love your neighbor as yourself."
James 2:8

Being Neighborly

How should I live among my non-Christian neighbors?

God's Response

If you see your neighbor's ox or sheep wandering away, don't pretend not to see it. Take it back to its owner. . . . Do the same if you find your neighbor's donkey, clothing, or anything else your neighbor loses.   *Deuteronomy 22:1, 3*

Be careful how you live among your unbelieving neighbors. Even if they accuse you of doing wrong, they will see your honorable behavior, and they will believe and give honor to God when he comes to judge the world.   *1 Peter 2:12*

I N OUR WORLD IT IS increasingly easy to say, "I don't want to get involved." When we see someone in need or notice something we could do to help, we may be tempted to turn a blind eye and pretend we don't notice. We may hope someone else will do something about it. God reminds us that his people are to be compassionate and active, ready and willing to go the extra mile as good neighbors.

God's Challenge

Accept each other just as Christ has accepted you; then God will be glorified.   *Romans 15:7*

Light of the World

How can I, as a Christian, have the greatest impact on my community?

God's Response

You must worship Christ as Lord of your life. And if you are asked about your Christian hope, always be ready to explain it. But you must do this in a gentle and respectful way. Keep your conscience clear. Then if people speak evil against you, they will be ashamed when they see what a good life you live because you belong to Christ. *1 Peter 3:15-16*

GOD'S INFLUENCE IN OUR LIVES IS often attractive to others. The more we reflect God's perfect character traits, the more people will be drawn to us and want to be around us (unless they are bent on evil). Although we all make plenty of mistakes, our goal should be for our neighbors to say, "We can plainly see that the Lord is with you." Would your neighbors say that about you?

God's Promise

You are the light of the world. . . . Don't hide your light under a basket! Instead, put it on a stand and let it shine for all. In the same way, let your good deeds shine out for all to see, so that everyone will praise your heavenly Father. *Matthew 5:14-16*

Strong Relationships

*How can I strengthen my relationships
with fellow believers?*

God's Response

Let us not neglect our meeting together, as some people
do, but encourage and warn each other, especially now
that the day of his coming back again is drawing near.
Hebrews 10:25

Paul went back to Galatia and Phrygia, visiting all the
believers, encouraging them and helping them to grow in
the Lord.   *Acts 18:23*

While Peter was in prison, the church prayed very earnestly
for him.   *Acts 12:5*

A COMMUNITY OF BELIEVERS PROVIDES an organized
way to hear the preaching and teaching of God's
Word. It is also an opportunity to get together with other
believers to strengthen, encourage, and build each other
up; pray for each other; hold each other accountable; and
meet one another's needs on a regular basis. God promises
to join you whenever you meet together.

God's Promise

Where two or three gather together because they are mine,
I am there among them.   *Matthew 18:20*

Foolishness

How does the Bible define foolishness?

God's Response

Only fools say in their hearts, "There is no God."
Psalm 14:1

Fear of the LORD is the beginning of knowledge. Only fools despise wisdom and discipline.   *Proverbs 1:7*

Fools have no interest in understanding; they only want to air their own opinions.   *Proverbs 18:2*

THE BIBLE DESCRIBES FOOLS as having one or more of the following characteristics: (1) refusing to acknowledge the existence of a loving God; (2) making no attempt to develop wisdom and self-discipline; (3) being entertained by making fun of what is good and moral; (4) speaking carelessly and thoughtlessly about others; and (5) thinking they are always right. Let "April Fool" describe just a day, not you!

God's Promise

Those who bring trouble on their families inherit only the wind. The fool will be a servant to the wise.
Proverbs 11:29

Wisdom

How does the Bible define wisdom?

God's Response

Reverence for the LORD is the foundation of true wisdom. The rewards of wisdom come to all who obey him.
Psalm 111:10

Pride leads to disgrace, but with humility comes wisdom.
Proverbs 11:2

A wise person is hungry for truth, while the fool feeds on trash. *Proverbs 15:14*

If you listen to constructive criticism, you will be at home among the wise. *Proverbs 15:31*

THE BIBLE STATES THAT REVERENCE for God is the foundation of true wisdom. If you revere and honor God, you will become humble, teachable, and hungry for truth. Reading God's Word will show you how to live. Immersing yourself in the truth of God will make you wise.

God's Promise

Wisdom will multiply your days and add years to your life. If you become wise, you will be the one to benefit. If you scorn wisdom, you will be the one to suffer.
Proverbs 9:11-12

Wisdom

How can I become wise?

God's Response

If you need wisdom—if you want to know what God wants you to do—ask him, and he will gladly tell you. He will not resent your asking.   *James 1:5*

Come here and listen to me! I'll pour out the spirit of wisdom upon you and make you wise.   *Proverbs 1:23*

Fear of the LORD is the beginning of wisdom. Knowledge of the Holy One results in understanding.   *Proverbs 9:10*

IF YOU WANT TO BE WISE, read and study God's Word and then do what it tells you. Knowing God's Word isn't enough; you must put it into practice. Solomon was known as the wisest man on earth, but when he stopped obeying God, wisdom left him (read 1 Kings 3:5-14; 9:4-9; 11:1-12). Your own thinking often leads to false assumptions, which then lead to unwise choices. Ask God for wisdom, that is, his perspective on things. Then your choices will be wise ones.

God's Promise

Trust in the LORD with all your heart; do not depend on your own understanding. Seek his will in all you do, and he will direct your paths.   *Proverbs 3:5-6*

Finding God

It's hard to see God in the everyday routine of life. How can I notice him?

God's Response

The humble will see their God at work and be glad. Let all who seek God's help live in joy.   *Psalm 69:32*

The LORD is close to all who call on him, yes, to all who call on him sincerely.   *Psalm 145:18*

The LORD went ahead of them. He guided them during the day with a pillar of cloud, and he provided light at night with a pillar of fire.   *Exodus 13:21 (NLT2)*

THERE ARE MANY WAYS TO see God's presence in our lives. Here are a few: (1) the evidence of God's work in creation; (2) the promises and the clear directions for life found in God's Word; (3) the evidence of God at work in the lives of others; (4) the assurance in your own heart that God is present; and (5) watching him redeem what is bad and make it good. If you don't notice God's presence in these things, you will not notice his presence even in a pillar of cloud or fire.

God's Promise

If you search for him with all your heart and soul, you will find him.   *Deuteronomy 4:29*

The Cross

What does the Cross represent?

God's Response

You know that God paid a ransom to save you. . . . He paid for you with the precious lifeblood of Christ, the sinless, spotless Lamb of God.   *1 Peter 1:18-19*

We know what real love is because Christ gave up his life for us.   *1 John 3:16*

IN OLD TESTAMENT DAYS, when a person brought an animal to the altar to be sacrificed, it symbolized the transfer of their sin to the animal. This allowed the person to be pure and holy before God again. In the New Testament, the cross is the altar and Jesus is the sacrifice. When he died on the cross, he transferred the sins of all people onto himself, forever. Jesus did this for you because he loves you. All you must do now is admit your sin to God and accept his forgiveness.

God's Promise

Now he has brought you back as his friends. He has done this through his death on the cross in his own human body. As a result, he has brought you into the very presence of God, and you are holy and blameless as you stand before him without a single fault.   *Colossians 1:22*

The Cross

Why did Jesus have to die on the cross?

God's Response

He personally carried away our sins in his own body on the cross so we can be dead to sin and live for what is right. You have been healed by his wounds!   *1 Peter 2:24*

He canceled the record that contained the charges against us. He took it and destroyed it by nailing it to Christ's cross.   *Colossians 2:14*

JESUS WANTS A RELATIONSHIP WITH YOU, but if your sin is not forgiven, that will separate you from him. Jesus' death was necessary to take away your guilt. When you believe and accept that Jesus did this for you, then you can begin to have a close relationship with him, which has been his plan since the beginning of time.

God's Promise

God in all his fullness was pleased to live in Christ, and by him God reconciled everything to himself. He made peace with everything in heaven and on earth by means of his blood on the cross. This includes you who were once so far away from God.   *Colossians 1:19-21*

Your Cross

What does the Cross mean for my life today?

God's Response

He gave his life to free us from every kind of sin, to cleanse us, and to make us his very own people, totally committed to doing what is right.   *Titus 2:14*

If any of you wants to be my follower . . . you must put aside your selfish ambition, shoulder your cross, and follow me.   *Mark 8:34*

IF THERE WERE NO CONSEQUENCES for driving through red lights, breaking into people's homes, or killing people, anarchy would reign. The things people value most—such as peace, order, and security—would be gone. Sin is breaking the laws that the Creator of the universe set up to maintain peace, order, and security in our world. Breaking God's laws brings God's punishment just as breaking government laws brings legal punishment. The good news is that when Jesus died on the cross, he took the punishment for sin that we deserved.

God's Promise

Those who belong to Christ Jesus have nailed the passions and desires of their sinful nature to his cross and crucified them there.   *Galatians 5:24*

Resurrection

Jesus' death was not the end, was it?

God's Response

You will not leave my soul among the dead or allow your godly one to rot in the grave.   *Psalm 16:10*

The angel spoke to the women. "Don't be afraid!" he said. "I know you are looking for Jesus, who was crucified. He isn't here! He has been raised from the dead, just as he said would happen. Come, see where his body was lying." *Matthew 28:5-6*

WITHOUT THE RESURRECTION of Jesus from the dead, there would be no Christianity. The Resurrection is central because it demonstrates God's power over death and assures us that we will also be resurrected. The power of God that brought Jesus back from the dead will also bring us back to life. Jesus' death was not the end. His resurrection is the beginning of eternal life for all who believe in him. Do you believe?

God's Promise

We know that God, who raised the Lord Jesus, will also raise us with Jesus and present us to himself together with you.   *2 Corinthians 4:14 (NLT2)*

Resurrection

What does Jesus' resurrection mean to me?

God's Response

God so loved the world that he gave his only Son, so that everyone who believes in him will not perish but have eternal life.   *John 3:16*

Our earthly bodies, which die and decay, will be different when they are resurrected, for they will never die. *1 Corinthians 15:42*

FAITH IN JESUS IS MEANINGLESS IF it does not last. Jesus' resurrection was the essential aspect of God's plan that allows you to spend eternity with him. Because Jesus was raised from the dead with a new body, you can be assured that he has the power over death and that you, too, will be resurrected one day with a new body and can live forever with him in heaven.

God's Promise

There are many rooms in my Father's home, and I am going to prepare a place for you. If this were not so, I would tell you plainly. When everything is ready, I will come and get you, so that you will always be with me where I am.   *John 14:2-3*

Resurrection

What will my body be like after it is resurrected?

God's Response

Our bodies now disappoint us, but when they are raised, they will be full of glory. They are weak now, but when they are raised, they will be full of power. They are natural human bodies now, but when they are raised, they will be spiritual bodies. For just as there are natural bodies, so also there are spiritual bodies.   *1 Corinthians 15:43-44*

YOUR RESURRECTED BODY will be a physical body like you have now, but it will also have many supernatural characteristics. You may be able to walk through walls as Jesus did with his resurrected body. Most importantly, your new body won't decay from the effects of sin. You will never be sick or in pain again, nor will your mind think sinful thoughts. You will be fully and finally perfect in God's sight.

God's Promise

We will not all die, but we will all be transformed! . . . Our mortal bodies must be transformed into immortal bodies.   *1 Corinthians 15:51, 53 (NLT2)*

Confidence

How can I have confidence that God will resurrect me someday?

God's Response

Tell me this—since we preach that Christ rose from the dead, why are some of you saying there will be no resurrection of the dead? For if there is no resurrection of the dead, then Christ has not been raised either. *1 Corinthians 15:12-13*

EYEWITNESS EVIDENCE FOR any historical event is the most reliable. Hundreds of eyewitnesses claimed to have seen Jesus following the Resurrection. The apostles were willing to risk martyrdom for preaching the truth about it, and millions upon millions of changed lives bear witness to the fact that Jesus rose from the dead and is alive today. Because of the Resurrection, we know that Christ's sacrifice on the cross accomplished God's plan of salvation—our sins are forgiven and we will live forever with Jesus in heaven. Christianity, at its heart, is not just another moral or religious code, but resurrection and new life.

God's Promise

I am the resurrection and the life. Those who believe in me, even though they die like everyone else, will live again. *John 11:25*

Hope

What is my hope and where does it come from?

God's Response

LORD, where do I put my hope? My only hope is in you.
Psalm 39:7

O Lord, you alone are my hope. I've trusted you, O LORD,
from childhood. *Psalm 71:5*

Through Christ you have come to trust in God. And
because God raised Christ from the dead and gave him
great glory, your faith and hope can be placed confidently
in God. *1 Peter 1:21*

THE LORD IS OUR SOURCE of hope because his promises are true. We lose hope when we stop believing
that. The Resurrection, the greatest event in history, is the
foundation of your hope. Jesus promised that he would
rise from the dead, and because he did, you can be assured
that every other promise God makes to you will also come
true.

God's Promise

You will have courage because you will have hope.
Job 11:18

Hope

Why should I trust God as my hope?

God's Response

God has given us both his promise and his oath. These two things are unchangeable because it is impossible for God to lie. Therefore, we who have fled to him for refuge can take new courage, for we can hold on to his promise with confidence. This confidence is like a strong and trustworthy anchor for our souls. It leads us through the curtain of heaven into God's inner sanctuary.
Hebrews 6:18-19

G OD CANNOT LIE BECAUSE HE IS TRUTH and he is the source of truth. God, therefore, cannot break his promises. Our greatest hope as followers of Jesus is that we will live in heaven with him just as he promised, with no more sin, pain, or suffering. You can find no greater guarantee. Now you can live each day with the confidence that things will happen as he says.

God's Promise

Without wavering, let us hold tightly to the hope we say we have, for God can be trusted to keep his promise.
Hebrews 10:23

Hopelessness

What can I do when things seem hopeless?

God's Response

Hannah was in deep anguish, crying bitterly as she prayed to the LORD.   *1 Samuel 1:10*

He took no chances but put them into the inner dungeon and clamped their feet in the stocks. Around midnight, Paul and Silas were praying and singing hymns to God. *Acts 16:24-25*

Wait patiently for the LORD. Be brave and courageous. *Psalm 27:14*

WHEN YOU LOSE HOPE, YOU DESPAIR. This will happen when you try to solve your problems by yourself. Hope returns when you remember that God is still in charge and that he has the power to change your life. When things seem hopeless, return to God, pray to him, praise him, and wait patiently and courageously for him to act on your behalf.

God's Promise

Happy are those who have the God of Israel as their helper, whose hope is in the LORD their God. *Psalm 146:5*

Hope

*How can I keep hoping when God
never seems to act?*

God's Response

Now that we are saved, we eagerly look forward to this
freedom. For if you already have something, you don't
need to hope for it.   *Romans 8:24*

What is faith? It is the confident assurance that what we
hope for is going to happen. It is the evidence of things
we cannot yet see.   *Hebrews 11:1*

When doubts filled my mind, your comfort gave me
renewed hope and cheer.   *Psalm 94:19*

HOPE, BY DEFINITION, is expecting something that has
not yet occurred. Faith and patience keep hope alive.
Have faith that God will do what he has promised, and be
patient while he does it in his own time and way. You can
be absolutely sure that he is already acting on your behalf
because God is trustworthy.

God's Promise

Hope in the LORD; for with the LORD there is
unfailing love and an overflowing supply of salvation.
Psalm 130:7

Hope

How can I cultivate stronger hope?

God's Response

Such things were written in the Scriptures long ago to teach us. They give us hope and encouragement as we wait patiently for God's promises.   *Romans 15:4*

Do not snatch your word of truth from me, for my only hope is in your laws. . . . May all who fear you find in me a cause for joy, for I have put my hope in your word. . . . I faint with longing for your salvation; but I have put my hope in your word. . . . You are my refuge and my shield; your word is my only source of hope. . . . I rise early, before the sun is up; I cry out for help and put my hope in your words.   *Psalm 119:43, 74, 81, 114, 147*

EVERY TIME YOU VISIT GOD'S WORD, your hope for his presence, comfort, rescue, and provision will be renewed and reinforced. His Word never fails or wavers. Cultivate stronger hope by reading and meditating on the promises of God's Word.

God's Promise

If we are faithful to the end, trusting God just as firmly as when we first believed, we will share in all that belongs to Christ.   *Hebrews 3:14*

God's Word

Can I truly trust the Bible as God's Word?

God's Response

All Scripture is inspired by God and is useful to teach us what is true and to make us realize what is wrong in our lives. It straightens us out and teaches us to do what is right.   *2 Timothy 3:16*

No prophecy in Scripture ever came from the prophets. . . . It was the Holy Spirit who moved the prophets to speak from God.   *2 Peter 1:20-21*

Not one word has failed of all the wonderful promises he gave through his servant Moses.   *1 Kings 8:56*

THE BIBLE HAS STOOD THE TEST of time better than any other document in human history. You can be sure that God protects the integrity of his Word, the Bible. He will not let his words disappear or be altered. God's Word lasts forever.

God's Promise

Forever, O LORD, your word stands firm in heaven. *Psalm 119:89*

God's Word

*How can a book written so long ago
be relevant for me today?*

God's Response

The word of God is full of living power. It is sharper than the sharpest knife, cutting deep into our innermost thoughts and desires. It exposes us for what we really are. *Hebrews 4:12*

Your words are what sustain me. They bring me great joy and are my heart's delight.   *Jeremiah 15:16*

Your promise revives me; it comforts me in all my troubles. *Psalm 119:50*

AS THE WORD OF GOD, the Bible is the only document that is "living," that is, relevant for all people in all places for all time. It is as contemporary as the heart of God and as powerful as your most urgent need. It will sustain you and bring you joy regardless of what happens in life because God uses it to speak to you.

God's Promise

The grass withers, and the flowers fade, but the word of our God stands forever.   *Isaiah 40:8*

God's Word

What will I experience when reading the Bible?

God's Response

I have not departed from his commands but have treasured his word in my heart.   *Job 23:12*

They are more desirable than gold. . . . They are sweeter than honey, even honey dripping from the comb.   *Psalm 19:10*

Encourage me by your word.   *Psalm 119:28*

Your principles have been the music of my life.
Psalm 119:54

YOU WILL BE SUCCESSFUL IN YOUR LIFE as a Christian when you commit yourself to vigorous spiritual training and preparation (Ephesians 6:10-18). Begin by reading God's Word consistently and inviting God to be part of your life every day. When you consistently obey God's Word, you will experience victory over your fears, over Satan's tactics to derail your relationship with God, and ultimately, over sin and death. You will then experience incredible joy.

God's Promise

Study this Book of the Law continually. Meditate on it day and night so you may be sure to obey all that is written in it. Only then will you succeed.   *Joshua 1:8*

Comfort

Can I find comfort in God's Word?

God's Response

I meditate on your age-old laws; O LORD, they comfort me.   *Psalm 119:52*

Whenever you were in distress and turned to the LORD . . . and sought him out, you found him.   *2 Chronicles 15:4*

The LORD is good. When trouble comes, he is a strong refuge. And he knows everyone who trusts in him.   *Nahum 1:7*

GOD DOESN'T ALWAYS ACT in the way we expect, because our expectations come from faulty human perceptions. Most of us expect God to comfort us by providing us with the things that we want or think we need, but the Bible says that God often comforts us with his presence, not with provisions. Things are temporary, but God is permanent and eternal. God shows up every time we need comfort, not with presents, but with his presence. This comfort is meaningful, lasting, and personal.

God's Promise

Don't be afraid, for I am with you. Do not be dismayed, for I am your God. I will strengthen you. I will help you. I will uphold you with my victorious right hand. *Isaiah 41:10*

Overwhelmed

I'm feeling completely overwhelmed.
How will God help me?

God's Response

I cry out to the LORD; I plead for the LORD's mercy. I pour out my complaints before him and tell him all my troubles. For I am overwhelmed, and you alone know the way I should turn.   *Psalm 142:1-3*

WE SOMETIMES FACE OVERWHELMING obstacles or opposition and feel outnumbered and helpless. God strengthens our confidence by reminding us that he has delivered his people in the past from their enemies and that he can deliver you from your troubles. True courage comes from knowing that God is stronger than your worst problem and that he wants to use his strength to help you. God promises to be with you, and his power is available to you when you are doing what pleases him.

God's Promise

The Sovereign LORD, the Holy One of Israel, says, "Only in returning to me and waiting for me will you be saved. In quietness and confidence is your strength." *Isaiah 30:15*

Overwhelmed

How do I cope when life's pain becomes overwhelming?

God's Response

Moses told the people, "Don't be afraid. Just stand where you are and watch the LORD rescue you." *Exodus 14:13*

Some wandered in the desert, lost and homeless. Hungry and thirsty, they nearly died. "LORD, help!" they cried in their trouble, and he rescued them from their distress. He led them straight to safety, to a city where they could live. Let them praise the LORD for his great love and for all his wonderful deeds to them. *Psalm 107:4-8*

WHEN WE TRY TO COPE WITH problems in our own strength, we can be overwhelmed. We soon recognize that we need someone bigger and stronger to help us. Our greatest source of help is almighty God, who accomplishes the impossible. When we focus on God, we become aware of his power and stop being preoccupied with ourselves. We can cope when God's strength replaces our weakness. Our impossibilities are God's opportunities.

God's Promise

He satisfies the thirsty and fills the hungry with good things. *Psalm 107:9*

Strength

What is the evidence of God's strength?
How strong is he?

God's Response

Who else has held the oceans in his hand? Who has measured off the heavens with his fingers? Who else knows the weight of the earth or has weighed out the mountains and the hills? . . . "To whom will you compare me? Who is my equal?" asks the Holy One. Look up into the heavens. Who created all the stars? He brings them out one after another, calling each by its name.   *Isaiah 40:12, 25-26*

The LORD opened up a path through the water with a strong east wind. The wind blew all that night, turning the seabed into dry land.   *Exodus 14:21*

GOD'S MIGHTY POWER IS evident in creation. God created and sustains the universe. He has named every star. The great message of the Bible is that this awesome and almighty God who parted the waters of the sea offers you his strength each day. Will you accept it?

God's Promise

The Sovereign LORD is my strength! He will make me as surefooted as a deer and bring me safely over the mountains.   *Habakkuk 3:19*

Strength

How can I experience God's strength in my life?

God's Response

I pray that you will begin to understand the incredible greatness of his power for us who believe him. This is the same mighty power that raised Christ from the dead. *Ephesians 1:19-20*

Glory be to God! By his mighty power at work within us, he is able to accomplish infinitely more than we would ever dare to ask or hope. May he be given glory in the church and in Christ Jesus forever and ever through endless ages. Amen. *Ephesians 3:20-21*

YOU EXPERIENCE GOD'S STRENGTH when you realize that you can tap into the same power that raised Jesus from the dead. God promises to infuse you with his strength when you depend on him. Each morning, ask God to give you strength for that day.

God's Promise

God has not given us a spirit of fear and timidity, but of power, love, and self-discipline. *2 Timothy 1:7*

Refinement

How does God's strength help me with my problems?

God's Response

There is wonderful joy ahead, even though it is necessary for you to endure many trials for a while. These trials are only to test your faith, to show that it is strong and pure. It is being tested as fire tests and purifies gold—and your faith is far more precious to God than mere gold. So if your faith remains strong after being tried by fiery trials, it will bring you much praise and glory and honor on the day when Jesus Christ is revealed to the whole world. *1 Peter 1:6-7*

THE NEXT TIME YOU FACE TROUBLE or hardship, see it as an opportunity to rely on God for strength and endurance. If you can trust him with your pain, confusion, and loneliness, you will win a spiritual victory. God never promised to make your life easy, but he did promise to be with you and to make your faith strong and pure through your trials.

God's Promise

Abraham never wavered in believing God's promise. In fact, his faith grew stronger, and in this he brought glory to God. *Romans 4:20*

Endurance

How can I become stronger in my faith?

God's Response

Dear brothers and sisters, whenever trouble comes your way, let it be an opportunity for joy. For when your faith is tested, your endurance has a chance to grow.   *James 1:2-3*

David continued, "Be strong and courageous, and do the work. Don't be afraid or discouraged by the size of the task, for the LORD God, my God, is with you. He will not fail you or forsake you."   *1 Chronicles 28:20*

FOLLOWING GOD DOESN'T make everything easy. In fact, the more important a task is, the more Satan will throw up roadblocks. If you know that God is leading you in a certain direction, don't give up just because the going gets tough. If anything, that should tell you that you are headed in the right direction. Keep moving forward boldly; your faith will be strengthened as you obey God in your life and in your daily choices. When you do this, you will be able to step out in stronger faith whenever God calls you.

God's Promise

The LORD is for me, so I will not be afraid. What can mere mortals do to me?   *Psalm 118:6*

Trouble

What should be my first response
when trouble comes?

God's Response

After Hezekiah received the letter and read it, he went up to the LORD's Temple and spread it out before the LORD. And Hezekiah prayed this prayer before the LORD: "O LORD Almighty, God of Israel, you are enthroned between the mighty cherubim! You alone are God of all the kingdoms of the earth. You alone created the heavens and the earth. Listen to me, O LORD, and hear! Open your eyes, O LORD, and see! . . . O LORD our God, rescue us." *Isaiah 37:14-17, 20*

WHEN TROUBLE COMES YOUR WAY, the first thing you should do is to bring the problem before God. Instead of jumping to conclusions, take time to discuss the problem with God and check your assumptions. When you assume the worst, act on bad advice, or refuse to admit that you have done something wrong, the problem will only become worse. Asking others for help, wisdom, and guidance is good, but only after you have asked God first.

God's Promise

I will call to you whenever trouble strikes, and you will answer me. *Psalm 86:7*

Standing Firm

After I've prayed about the trouble I'm facing, then what?

God's Response

When they arrived [Paul] declared, "You know that from the day I set foot in the province of Asia until now I have done the Lord's work humbly. . . . Yet I never shrank from telling you the truth, either publicly or in your homes. . . . And now I am going to Jerusalem, drawn there irresistibly by the Holy Spirit, not knowing what awaits me, except that the Holy Spirit has told me in city after city that jail and suffering lie ahead. But my life is worth nothing unless I use it for doing the work assigned me by the Lord Jesus— the work of telling others the Good News about God's wonderful kindness and love." *Acts 20:18-20, 22-24*

STAND FIRM IN OBEDIENCE. Paul talked to God about the trouble that awaited him, but he still stepped forward. When trouble comes, continue to do what you know is right. The greatest blessing of obedience is God's presence, and that is what will help you through to the other side of your difficulties.

God's Promise

Do what is right and good in the LORD's sight, so all will go well with you. *Deuteronomy 6:18*

Endurance

*Where do I find the strength to keep going
when I'm tempted to give up?*

God's Response

Endure suffering along with me, as a good soldier of
Christ Jesus.   *2 Timothy 2:3*

Of course, you get no credit for being patient if you are
beaten for doing wrong. But if you suffer for doing right
and are patient beneath the blows, God is pleased with
you.   *1 Peter 2:20*

YOUR OUTLOOK ON LIFE DETERMINES how you see your
problems. If you see them only as nuisances, you will
develop an attitude of bitterness, cynicism, and hopelessness that will make you want to give up. If you see your
problems as an opportunity for strengthening your character and convictions, you will be able to rise above them
and persevere to see what good things God has in store for
you. Endurance is a sign that your faith is growing strong.

God's Promise

Christ, the faithful Son, was in charge of the entire
household. And we are God's household, if we keep up
our courage and remain confident in our hope in Christ.
Hebrews 3:6

Courage

How do I develop endurance?

God's Response

Let us run with endurance the race that God has set before us. We do this by keeping our eyes on Jesus, on whom our faith depends from start to finish. He was willing to die a shameful death on the cross because of the joy he knew would be his afterward. Now he is seated in the place of highest honor beside God's throne in heaven. Think about all he endured when sinful people did such terrible things to him, so that you don't become weary and give up. *Hebrews 12:1-3*

C OURAGE IS THE ABILITY TO act in accordance with what we know to be right and good in spite of threat or danger. Endurance is the ability to be courageous again and again. Christians recognize that they can endure only because of God's promised help in time of need. This should make us bold in facing any situation that comes our way.

God's Promise

Use every piece of God's armor to resist the enemy in the time of evil, so that after the battle you will still be standing firm. *Ephesians 6:13*

Renewal

Spring makes me think of new life and renewal.
In what ways can God renew me?

God's Response

In its place you have clothed yourselves with a brand-new nature that is continually being renewed as you learn more and more about Christ, who created this new nature within you.   *Colossians 3:10*

M OST OF US WILL ADMIT THAT we are not the people we really want to be. We're not as disciplined, thoughtful, productive, loving, or caring as we would like. In fact, some parts of our lives don't just need tinkering; they need a fresh start. When you become a follower of Jesus, he promises the renewal that brings peace, joy, and a whole new perspective on life. Jesus offers to redeem your thoughts, attitudes, habits, regrets, and relationships. You can become, over time, the kind of person that God wants you to be and that you, deep down, want to be as well.

God's Promise

I long to obey your commandments! Renew my life with your goodness. . . . I will never forget your commandments, for you have used them to restore my joy and health.   *Psalm 119:40, 93*

Renewal

How can I experience renewal in my life?

God's Response

When I refused to confess my sin, I was weak and miserable, and I groaned all day long. Day and night your hand of discipline was heavy on me. My strength evaporated like water in the summer heat. . . . Finally, I confessed all my sins to you and stopped trying to hide them. I said to myself, "I will confess my rebellion to the Lord." And you forgave me! All my guilt is gone. *Psalm 32:3-5*

ONE OF THE FIRST IMPORTANT STEPS toward renewal is confession, which means being humbly honest with God and sincerely sorry for your sins—the ones you know about and the ones you are unaware of. Confession restores your relationship with God, and this renews your strength and spirit. When you repent, God removes your guilt, restores your joy, and heals your broken soul. A heart that truly longs for change is ready for the renewal that only God's Spirit can bring.

God's Promise

Turn from your sins and turn to God, so you can be cleansed of your sins. *Acts 3:19*

Prayer

What is prayer?

God's Response

I confess my sins; I am deeply sorry for what I have done. *Psalm 38:18*

The priest said, "Let's ask God first." *1 Samuel 14:36*

I will thank you, LORD, with all my heart. . . . I will sing praises to your name, O Most High. *Psalm 9:1-2*

The next morning Jesus awoke long before daybreak and went out alone into the wilderness to pray. *Mark 1:35*

PRAYER IS TALKING TO GOD and building a relationship with him. As you talk to him, you praise and thank him, make requests, confess sins, express pain and frustration, and simply share what is happening in your life. Good conversation also includes listening, so make time for God to speak to you. When you listen to God, he can make his wisdom and resources available to you. Prayer can also soften your heart and help you to avoid the debilitating effects of anger, resentment, and bitterness.

God's Promise

The eyes of the Lord watch over those who do right, and his ears are open to their prayers. *1 Peter 3:12*

Prayer Power

Why is prayer important?

God's Response

Keep on asking, and you will be given what you ask for. Keep on looking, and you will find. Keep on knocking, and the door will be opened. For everyone who asks, receives. Everyone who seeks, finds. And the door is opened to everyone who knocks. You parents—if your children ask for a loaf of bread, do you give them a stone instead? Or if they ask for a fish, do you give them a snake? Of course not! If you sinful people know how to give good gifts to your children, how much more will your heavenly Father give good gifts to those who ask him. *Matthew 7:7-11*

GOD OFTEN WORKS MORE in your own heart through the act of prayer than he does in actually answering your prayer. Your prayers are often self-centered, and God changes your heart to be more other-centered. As you persist in asking, seeking, and knocking, you often gain greater understanding of yourself, your situation, your motivation, and God's nature and direction for your life.

God's Promise

The earnest prayer of a righteous person has great power and wonderful results.   *James 5:16*

God Hears

MAY 5

How can I know that God hears my prayers?

God's Response

When they pray . . . hear from heaven . . . and grant what they ask of you. In this way, all the people of the earth will come to know and fear you.   *2 Chronicles 6:32-33 (NLT2)*

If my people who are called by my name will humble themselves and pray and seek my face and turn from their wicked ways, I will hear from heaven.   *2 Chronicles 7:14*

The LORD is far from the wicked, but he hears the prayers of the righteous.   *Proverbs 15:29*

SOMETIMES IT SEEMS THAT our prayers are bouncing off the ceiling. Is God not paying attention? The bigger question is, are you paying attention to God's answer? God does answer prayer, and he wants to do so because he is loving and good. It is his nature to give good things to his people. Sometimes, after things work out, we fail to give God the credit. When you pray, be alert and watch for God's answer, and then don't forget to thank him for it!

God's Promise

If we know he is listening when we make our requests, we can be sure that he will give us what we ask for.
1 John 5:15

Answered Prayer

Does God always answer prayer?

God's Response

Three different times I begged the Lord to take it away. Each time he said, . . . "My power works best in your weakness." *2 Corinthians 12:8-9*

If you stay joined to me and my words remain in you, you may ask any request you like, and it will be granted! *John 15:7*

GOD LISTENS CAREFULLY to every prayer and answers it. His answer may be yes, no, or wait, not now. Doesn't any loving parent give all three of these responses to a child? Answering yes to every request would spoil you and be dangerous to your well-being. Answering no to every request would be vindictive, stingy, and kill our spirit. Answering wait to every prayer would be frustrating. God always answers, but he gives his answers based on what he knows is best for you. When you don't get the answer you want, your spiritual maturity will grow as you seek to understand why God's answer is in your best interest.

God's Promise

The eyes of the Lord watch over those who do right, and his ears are open to their prayers. *1 Peter 3:12*

Intercession

Does it make a difference when others are praying for me or when I am praying for others?

God's Response

He will rescue us because you are helping by praying for us.
2 Corinthians 1:11

The earnest prayer of a righteous person has great power and wonderful results.   *James 5:16*

PAUL WAS CONVINCED THAT the Corinthians' prayers vitally influenced his deliverance by God. Intercession is praying for the needs of others. It is easy to become discouraged if you think that there is nothing anyone can do for you—or nothing that you can do to help someone you care about. But the most important thing that you can do for others, and others can do for you, is to pray. In ways beyond our understanding, intercessory prayer creates a channel into which the love and power of God can be released, as well as creating a deep bond of fellowship between human beings. Intercession is thus a vital source of hope and help.

God's Promise

We fasted and earnestly prayed that our God would take care of us, and he heard our prayer.   *Ezra 8:23*

Prayer

What does God want in my communication with him?

God's Response

O my people, trust in him at all times. Pour out your heart to him, for God is our refuge. *Psalm 62:8*

Devote yourselves to prayer with an alert mind and a thankful heart. *Colossians 4:2*

Father, if you are willing, please take this cup of suffering away from me. Yet I want your will, not mine. *Luke 22:42*

GOD HONORS THE HUMBLE and acknowledges their prayers (1 Peter 5:6; Daniel 10:12). Humility comes when you recognize that you need God. Before you move out boldly, fall to your knees humbly. When you come to God in humility, your prayers will be more aligned with his plans for you because you will recognize God's sovereignty. His will for your life will lead you toward what is good and right and away from sin and harm.

God's Promise

I think how much you have helped me; I sing for joy in the shadow of your protecting wings. I follow close behind you; your strong right hand holds me securely. *Psalm 63:7-8*

Communication

How does God communicate with me?

God's Response

Get a scroll, and write down all my messages against Israel, Judah, and the other nations.   *Jeremiah 36:2*

Long ago God spoke many times and in many ways to our ancestors through the prophets. But now in these final days, he has spoken to us through his Son.   *Hebrews 1:1-2*

All that the Father has is mine; this is what I mean when I say that the Spirit will reveal to you whatever he receives from me.   *John 16:15*

GOD COMMUNICATES THROUGH HIS WORD, so it is wise to read it daily. He communicates through his Son, Jesus, so it is essential to talk to him daily. He communicates through the Holy Spirit, so take regular quiet time to listen to the Spirit's counsel in your heart.

God's Promise

In earlier days he permitted all the nations to go their own ways, but he never left himself without a witness. There were always his reminders, such as sending you rain and good crops and giving you food and joyful hearts.   *Acts 14:16-17*

Words

When I speak to God and to others, do my words really matter?

God's Response

If you claim to be religious but don't control your tongue, you are just fooling yourself, and your religion is worthless. *James 1:26*

A gentle answer turns away wrath, but harsh words stir up anger. *Proverbs 15:1*

WHAT COMES OUT OF YOUR MOUTH shows what is in your heart. Your words show what kind of person you really are. Criticism, gossip, flattery, lying, and profanity are not only "word problems," but "heart problems" as well. Being more careful with your words isn't enough. You must first have a change of heart, and then good, kind, and healing words will follow.

God's Promise

Who may worship in your sanctuary, LORD? Who may enter your presence on your holy hill? Those who lead blameless lives and do what is right, speaking the truth from sincere hearts. Those who refuse to slander others or harm their neighbors or speak evil of their friends. *Psalm 15:1-3*

Affirmation

Why is it so important to affirm others?

God's Response

Encourage each other and build each other up, just as you are already doing. . . . Think highly of them and give them your wholehearted love because of their work. And remember to live peaceably with each other. . . . Encourage those who are timid. Take tender care of those who are weak.   *1 Thessalonians 5:11, 13-14*

E VERY PERSON HAS A GOD-GIVEN need to be affirmed. You can give the gift of affirmation through three actions: (1) Listen. Listening bestows dignity by putting another person at the center of your attention. (2) Encourage. Encouraging others is a powerful way to build up their confidence and motivate them for even better work. (3) Act. Following through on someone's suggestion makes a strong statement about your respect for them. Who needs your affirmation today?

God's Challenge

The whole law can be summed up in this one command: "Love your neighbor as yourself." But if instead of showing love among yourselves you are always biting and devouring one another, watch out! Beware of destroying one another.   *Galatians 5:14-15*

Affirmation

How does God affirm me?

God's Response

May God be merciful and bless us. May his face shine with favor upon us.   *Psalm 67:1*

I passed on to you what was most important and what had also been passed on to me—that Christ died for our sins, just as the Scriptures said.   *1 Corinthians 15:3*

GOD AFFIRMS YOU IN MANY WAYS. (1) He loves you so much that he has provided a way for you to live forever with him. (2) He blesses you with the beauty of his creation, through friends, family, and other believers, and by giving you talents and spiritual gifts. (3) He grants you mercy. He sees such value in you that he offers you the free gift of salvation. What greater affirmation can you receive than to have the most important Being in the universe pay such personal attention to you?

God's Promise

Now God is building you, as living stones, into his spiritual temple. What's more, you are God's holy priests, who offer the spiritual sacrifices that please him because of Jesus Christ.   *1 Peter 2:5*

Value

Am I really that important to God?

God's Response

God said, "Let us make people in our image, to be like ourselves." *Genesis 1:26*

You should not be like cowering, fearful slaves. You should behave instead like God's very own children, adopted into his family—calling him "Father, dear Father." For his Holy Spirit speaks to us deep in our hearts and tells us that we are God's children. And since we are his children, we will share his treasures—for everything God gives to his Son, Christ, is ours, too. *Romans 8:15-17*

YOU MAY BE TEMPTED TO measure your value on the basis of your performance or other external measurements, but your worth is rooted in the fact that you are created in God's image and loved as God's child. He loved you enough to die for you. That's how important you are to him!

God's Promise

Not even a sparrow, worth only half a penny, can fall to the ground without your Father knowing it. . . . You are more valuable to him than a whole flock of sparrows. *Matthew 10:29, 31*

Self-Esteem

How can I develop healthy self-esteem?

God's Response

Be honest in your estimate of yourselves, measuring your value by how much faith God has given you.
Romans 12:3

God has given gifts to each of you. . . . Manage them well so that God's generosity can flow through you.
1 Peter 4:10

HEALTHY SELF-ESTEEM COMES from an honest appraisal of yourself—not too proud, because your gifts and abilities were given to you by God, yet not so self-effacing that you fail to use your gifts and abilities to their potential. Using your gifts to bless and serve others actually increases your self-worth because it takes the focus off of yourself and allows God to work more effectively through you.

God's Promise

How precious are your thoughts about me, O God!
Psalm 139:17

Beauty

I don't feel very beautiful. What does God consider beautiful?

God's Response

You should be known for the beauty that comes from within, the unfading beauty of a gentle and quiet spirit, which is so precious to God.   *1 Peter 3:4*

SOME OF US ARE MORE BEAUTIFUL than others; that's a fact of life on this earth. Fortunately, God's definition of beauty is inside out from ours. He makes it clear that the beauty that matters most is not based on the appearance of our body or face, but on the condition of our heart. In this world, those with beautiful looks often have an advantage, but in the world to come, those with beautiful hearts will be seen as the pinnacle of God's creation. The more your heart reflects the beauty of God's character now, the more beautiful you are becoming for life in God's eternal kingdom. Such inner beauty will not go unnoticed here on earth, either!

God's Promise

Charm is deceptive, and beauty does not last; but a woman who fears the LORD will be greatly praised.
Proverbs 31:30

Beauty

How can my words and actions be beautiful?

God's Response

The LORD despises the thoughts of the wicked, but he delights in pure words.   *Proverbs 15:26*

Timely advice is as lovely as golden apples in a silver basket.   *Proverbs 25:11*

Women who claim to be devoted to God should make themselves attractive by the good things they do. *1 Timothy 2:10*

BEAUTIFUL WORDS AND ACTIONS are the result of godly thoughts and character. When you spend most of your time thinking about what is good and right, your words and actions will be mostly good and right. Just as you must practice a hobby or sport to be good at it, you must practice thinking about what is good for it to become a habit. Make a list of the good things you can think about this week.

God's Challenge

Whatever you do or say, let it be as a representative of the Lord Jesus, all the while giving thanks through him to God the Father.   *Colossians 3:17*

Empowerment

I want to live as God's representative.
How does he help me to obey him?

God's Response

You must be even more careful to put into action God's saving work in your lives, obeying God with deep reverence and fear. For God is working in you, giving you the desire to obey him and the power to do what pleases him.   *Philippians 2:12-13*

If you love me, obey my commandments. And I will ask the Father, and he will give you another Counselor, who will never leave you.   *John 14:15-16*

G OD EMPOWERS US FOR THE THINGS that he requires of us. You can obey him because he gives you his Holy Spirit to help you. Even as the air you breathe empowers your body to function, so the Holy Spirit empowers your spirit to obey. God's Word releases you from bondage to sin so that you are free to obey him.

God's Promise

If you keep looking steadily into God's perfect law—the law that sets you free—and if you do what it says and don't forget what you heard, then God will bless you for doing it.   *James 1:25*

God's Promises

What does God promise to those who obey him?

God's Response

Oh, the joys of those who do not follow the advice of the wicked, or stand around with sinners, or join in with scoffers. But they delight in doing everything the LORD wants; day and night they think about his law. They are like trees planted along the riverbank, bearing fruit each season without fail. Their leaves never wither, and in all they do, they prosper.   *Psalm 1:1-3*

O BEDIENCE IS THE WAY to abundant life. When you obey, you have a clear conscience and uninterrupted friendship with the Lord. You honor other people and stay out of trouble. Your priorities become clear and you don't waste time or energy in unprofitable ways. As a river flows freely through an unblocked channel, God's grace and provision flow through you when you follow his ways.

God's Promise

No good thing will the LORD withhold from those who do what is right.   *Psalm 84:11*

Holiness

What does it mean to be holy and to live a holy life?

God's Response

Your sins have been washed away, and you have been set apart for God.   *1 Corinthians 6:11*

I plead with you to give your bodies to God. Let them be a living and holy sacrifice—the kind he will accept. *Romans 12:1*

THINK OF HOLINESS AS BOTH a journey and a final destination. To be completely holy is to be sinless, pure, and perfect before God. Of course, none of us is perfect, so that is our ultimate goal, our final destination when we stand before God in heaven. But holiness also means to be different, to be "set apart" by God for a specific purpose. We are to be different from the rest of the world, and our lives are a journey toward becoming a little bit more pure and sinless with each passing day. If you strive to be holy during your earthly journey, you will one day arrive at your final destination to stand holy before God.

God's Promise

[Christ] is the one who made us acceptable to God. He made us pure and holy.   *1 Corinthians 1:30*

Set Apart

Does God really expect me to be holy?
How is that possible?

God's Response

Who can create purity in one born impure?   *Job 14:4*

I, the LORD, am holy, and I make you holy.   *Leviticus 21:8*

He gave up his life for [the church] to make her holy
and clean . . . to present her to himself as a glorious
church without a spot or wrinkle or any other blemish.
Ephesians 5:25-27

TO BE HOLY SIMPLY MEANS to live a life that is pure,
blameless, and single-heartedly devoted to what God
calls us to. This means that we need to live by the standard of conduct that God teaches us in the Bible, and
not blindly follow what everyone around us is doing. As
followers of Jesus, we live a holy life because we want to
please God and because our example can influence others
to follow him. How can you live a more holy life today
than yesterday?

God's Promise

Long ago, even before he made the world, God loved us
and chose us in Christ to be holy and without fault in
his eyes.   *Ephesians 1:4*

Thought Life

How are my actions affected by my thoughts?

God's Response

With the Lord's authority let me say this: Live no longer as the ungodly do, for they are hopelessly confused. . . . They don't care anymore about right and wrong, and they have given themselves over to immoral ways. Their lives are filled with all kinds of impurity and greed. . . . Instead, there must be a spiritual renewal of your thoughts and attitudes. You must display a new nature because you are a new person, created in God's likeness—righteous, holy, and true.   *Ephesians 4:17, 19, 23-24*

THE SEEDS OF YOUR ACTIONS, both good and bad, are planted in your mind and heart. If you want your actions to be godly, then nurture godly thoughts. It is helpful to meditate on good and pure things as soon as any bad thoughts come to mind. By immediately focusing on God, you can replace bad thoughts with good ones. It is worthwhile to keep your mind pure so you won't gradually be lured into darkness and confusion.

God's Promise

You will keep in perfect peace all who trust in you, whose thoughts are fixed on you!   *Isaiah 26:3*

Thought Life

How can my thought life be pleasing to God?

God's Response

Fix your thoughts on what is true and honorable and right. Think about things that are pure and lovely and admirable. Think about things that are excellent and worthy of praise.   *Philippians 4:8*

CONTROLLING OUR THOUGHT LIVES is one of our greatest struggles. God takes your thought life very seriously, because your thoughts define and disclose who you really are. Even if you do not act them out immediately or exactly, thoughts shape your attitudes and actions. A habit of ungodly thinking easily leads to a habit of sinful living. We are to allow God to change the way we think by focusing our thoughts on him, and on anything that is true, honorable, right, pure, lovely, admirable, excellent, and worthy of praise. We can begin with reading, meditating on, and memorizing Scripture that focuses on these good things.

God's Promise

I know, my God, that you examine our hearts and rejoice when you find integrity there.   *1 Chronicles 29:17*

Discipline

How can I discipline my mind?

God's Response

I will reject perverse ideas and stay away from every evil.
Psalm 101:4

"But this is the new covenant I will make with the people of Israel on that day," says the LORD. "I will put my laws in their minds, and I will write them on their hearts. I will be their God, and they will be my people."   *Jeremiah 31:33*

GOD HAS PROMISED A NEW HEART and a new mind to those who follow him. A new mind is no longer controlled by sinful thoughts, but by the Holy Spirit. As you grow in your understanding and experience of God's holiness with the help of the Holy Spirit, you will become increasingly sensitive to sin. Then you will want God to change your thought life in a way that reflects him.

God's Promise

Let the people turn from their wicked deeds. Let them banish from their minds the very thought of doing wrong! Let them turn to the LORD that he may have mercy on them. Yes, turn to our God, for he will abundantly pardon.   *Isaiah 55:7*

Mind of Christ

The Bible says I have the "mind of Christ."
What does that mean?

God's Response

"Who can know what the Lord is thinking? Who can give him counsel?" But we can understand these things, for we have the mind of Christ.   *1 Corinthians 2:16*

You are controlled by the Spirit if you have the Spirit of God living in you.   *Romans 8:9*

YOU HAVE THE MIND OF CHRIST because, through the guidance of the Holy Spirit, you have insight into God's purpose and plan for his people. You are able to invite the Holy Spirit into your thought life to give you wisdom and discernment that is not available to those who don't belong to God. God also speaks to your spirit as you read the Bible and talk to him in prayer.

God's Promise

This is the new covenant I will make with my people on that day, says the Lord: I will put my laws in their hearts so they will understand them, and I will write them on their minds so they will obey them.   *Hebrews 10:16*

Christlikeness

In what other ways can I become like Christ?

God's Response

All of us have had that veil removed so that we can be mirrors that brightly reflect the glory of the Lord. And as the Spirit of the Lord works within us, we become more and more like him and reflect his glory even more. *2 Corinthians 3:18*

We will hold to the truth in love, becoming more and more in every way like Christ, who is the head of his body, the church. *Ephesians 4:15*

I myself no longer live, but Christ lives in me. So I live my life in this earthly body by trusting in the Son of God, who loved me and gave himself for me. *Galatians 2:20*

WHEN YOU TRUST IN JESUS CHRIST for salvation, the Holy Spirit begins to work in your heart to make you more and more like Jesus. You can cooperate with this process by carefully studying how Jesus lived and loved, what he taught, and how he treated others. Invite him to work in you and watch the amazing transformation from his powerful love.

God's Promise

I have given you an example to follow. *John 13:15*

The Past

What if I have a lot of pain in my past?
How can I deal with that?

God's Response

Esau ran to meet him and embraced him affectionately and kissed him. Both of them were in tears.   *Genesis 33:4*

Jesus said, "Father, forgive these people, because they don't know what they are doing."   *Luke 23:34*

If you are standing before the altar in the Temple, offering a sacrifice to God, and you suddenly remember that someone has something against you, leave your sacrifice there beside the altar. Go and be reconciled to that person. Then come and offer your sacrifice to God. *Matthew 5:23-24*

FORGIVENESS IS BOTH a decision and a process. Sometimes you must decide to forgive before your feelings of mercy and forgiveness happen. As you release the hurt inflicted on you, you will be healed and freed to grow beyond the pain. Is there someone you need to forgive so that you can move forward?

God's Promise

Forgive us our sins, just as we have forgiven those who have sinned against us.   *Matthew 6:12*

Revenge

How can I deal with a hurtful past?

God's Response

Be kind to each other, tenderhearted, forgiving one another, just as God through Christ has forgiven you. *Ephesians 4:32*

I will forgive their wrongdoings, and I will never again remember their sins.   *Hebrews 8:12*

S OMETIMES WE FEEL THAT if we can forgive, then we can forget. Forgiveness is not really about forgetting (which is often impossible), but about surrendering your right to hurt another person back. Forgiveness allows you to release the bitter desire for retribution and frees you from anger, hurt, and bitterness. After someone has wronged you, time will either harden your heart, making you bitter and unyielding, or it will soften it, giving you a desire for healing and restoration. Willingness to forgive is the only way to achieve these.

God's Challenge

No, dear brothers and sisters, I am still not all I should be, but I am focusing all my energies on this one thing: Forgetting the past and looking forward to what lies ahead.   *Philippians 3:13*

Remembrance

What are some good things I should remember about the past?

God's Response

We will not hide these truths from our children but will tell the next generation about the glorious deeds of the LORD. We will tell of his power and the mighty miracles he did. . . . So each generation can set its hope anew on God, remembering his glorious miracles and obeying his commands.   *Psalm 78:4, 7*

Sing to him; yes, sing his praises. Tell everyone about his miracles. . . . Think of the wonderful works he has done, the miracles and the judgments he handed down. *Psalm 105:2, 5*

NEVER FORGET WHAT GOD has done for you. Share God's faithfulness—both in your life and in the lives of others—with your friends, family, children, and grand-children, so that you will build a testimony for future generations.

God's Challenge

Will not even one of you apply these lessons from the past?   *Isaiah 42:23*

Legacy

How can I make lasting memories of God's work in my life?

God's Response

We will use these stones to build a memorial. In the future, your children will ask, "What do these stones mean to you?" Then you can tell them.   *Joshua 4:6-7*

THE BIBLE IS THE RECORD of God's work in history. Reading it reminds us and our children of who God is and what he has done. As the Israelites set up stones to remind them of God's miraculous parting of the Jordan River, we can find creative ways to remind ourselves and our families of God's special work in our lives and in the lives of those who have gone before us. We can celebrate special anniversaries, write spiritual journals, sing worship songs, or tell stories of memory-laden objects to remind us of God's blessing in our lives. What are you doing today to show God's faithfulness to future generations?

God's Promise

God said, "I am giving you a sign as evidence of my eternal covenant with you and all living creatures. I have placed my rainbow in the clouds. It is the sign of my permanent promise to you and to all the earth."
Genesis 9:12-13

Blessings

What kinds of blessings can I expect from God?

God's Response

May the LORD bless you and protect you. May the LORD smile on you and be gracious to you. May the LORD show you his favor and give you his peace. *Numbers 6:24-26*

May grace and peace be yours, sent to you from God our Father and Jesus Christ our Lord. *Ephesians 1:2*

G OD'S BLESSINGS ARE EVERYWHERE, but we need spiritual eyes to see them as his gifts and not merely as luck or good fortune. His blessings come to you every day, in every conceivable form. Success and prosperity are usually not the most common blessings from God, for they tend to take our minds off of him. Rather, his presence, the beauty of creation, peace of heart, joy, spiritual gifts, family, friends, comfort, and hope are some of the best blessings he gives. The greatest blessing God wants to give is salvation and eternal life. We just need to ask for it.

God's Promise

Your goodness is so great! You have stored up great blessings for those who honor you. You have done so much for those who come to you for protection, blessing them before the watching world. *Psalm 31:19*

Being a Blessing

How can I be a blessing to others?

God's Response

We always thank God for all of you and pray for you constantly.   *1 Thessalonians 1:2*

Thanks be to God, who . . . leads us along in Christ's triumphal procession. Now wherever we go he uses us to tell others about the Lord and to spread the Good News like a sweet perfume.   *2 Corinthians 2:14*

W E BLESS OTHERS BY PRAYING FOR THEM, thanking God for them, and even by reciting Scripture verses such as these in their presence. When you spend time with others and share how God has worked in your life, they are blessed because they know that you care enough to seek God's favor for them. As you pass on the blessings God has poured on you, you bless others both physically and spiritually. Encouraging others with God's Good News is the best way to bless them forever.

God's Promise

All who are victorious will inherit all these blessings. *Revelation 21:7*

Refreshment

*How can the promise of blessing help me
when I am weary or discouraged?*

God's Response

How we thank God, who gives us victory over sin and
death through Jesus Christ our Lord! So, my dear brothers
and sisters, be strong and steady, always enthusiastic about
the Lord's work, for you know that nothing you do for the
Lord is ever useless.   *1 Corinthians 15:57-58*

Happy are those who are strong in the LORD, who set
their minds on a pilgrimage to Jerusalem. When they walk
through the Valley of Weeping, it will become a place of
refreshing springs, where pools of blessing collect after the
rains! They will continue to grow stronger, and each of
them will appear before God in Jerusalem.   *Psalm 84:5-7*

WHEN YOU ARE TEMPTED to give up, new resolve can
come from remembering that God promises to
strengthen you and to bring a harvest of blessing in his
perfect time. Nothing you do for God is ever wasted, and
nothing you endure is useless.

God's Promise

God blesses the people who patiently endure testing.
James 1:12

Strength

Can God use me when I feel so useless?

God's Response

Moses pleaded with the LORD, "O LORD, I'm just not a good speaker. I never have been, and I'm not now, even after you have spoken to me. I'm clumsy with words."

"Who makes mouths?" the LORD asked him. . . . "I will help you speak well, and I will tell you what to say." *Exodus 4:10-12*

In your strength I can crush an army; with my God I can scale any wall. *Psalm 18:29*

THERE ARE NO LIMITS TO what God can do in and through you. In his strength you have power to do things you could never do on your own. You can withstand the toughest attacks and take the offensive in overcoming your problems; you can live without fear because God's strength drives out fear. Give what you are to him and let him give you his strength.

God's Promise

I can do everything with the help of Christ who gives me the strength I need. *Philippians 4:13*

Exhaustion

Am I disappointing God by my tiredness?

God's Response

Jacob's well was there; and Jesus, tired from the long walk, sat wearily beside the well about noontime.   *John 4:6*

We grow weary in our present bodies, and we long for the day when we will put on our heavenly bodies. *2 Corinthians 5:2*

My gracious favor is all you need. My power works best in your weakness.   *2 Corinthians 12:9*

GOD MADE YOU A FLESH-AND-BLOOD human being. He lived in a human body, so he understands what it means to be tired. When you are exhausted, God cares for you like a tender parent who carries a sleeping child to bed. Your weariness can make you more aware of God's faithfulness. Take the rest you need, and trust him to work through your weakness.

God's Promise

Jesus said, "Come to me, all of you who are weary and carry heavy burdens, and I will give you rest." *Matthew 11:28*

Rest

What is God's prescription for my tiredness?

God's Response

On the seventh day, having finished his task, God rested from all his work. And God blessed the seventh day and declared it holy, because it was the day when he rested from his work of creation.   *Genesis 2:2-3*

It is useless for you to work so hard from early morning until late at night, anxiously working for food to eat; for God gives rest to his loved ones.   *Psalm 127:2*

Jesus said, "Let's get away from the crowds for a while and rest." There were so many people coming and going that Jesus and his apostles didn't even have time to eat.   *Mark 6:31*

GOD WANTS YOU TO TAKE A BREAK and get some rest! He set aside a full day of rest at creation as an example for us to follow. Jesus understood the limitations of his disciples and took them away for a break. Work is good, but it must be balanced by regular attention to the health of your body and your soul. Whole life comes from holy rest.

God's Challenge

Keep my Sabbath days of rest and show reverence toward my sanctuary, for I am the LORD.   *Leviticus 19:30*

Refreshment

*How can I experience true refreshment
in my times of rest?*

God's Response

[The Sabbath] is a permanent sign of my covenant with them. For in six days the LORD made heaven and earth, but he rested on the seventh day and was refreshed. *Exodus 31:17*

The LORD replied, "I will personally go with you, Moses. I will give you rest—everything will be fine for you." *Exodus 33:14*

I lay down and slept. I woke up in safety, for the LORD was watching over me. *Psalm 3:5*

R EST IS ONLY REFRESHING WHEN YOU truly set aside your work and your worries. Rest is physically, mentally, and psychologically refreshing; a healthy body, mind, and emotions make us more productive. Rest is also spiritually refreshing; a healthy soul allows us to focus fully on God. Above all, rest reminds us that we depend on God's provision, not on our own efforts.

God's Promise

God gives rest to his loved ones. *Psalm 127:2*

Refreshment

In what ways can my soul be refreshed?

God's Response

I thirst for God, the living God. When can I come and stand before him?   *Psalm 42:2*

O God, you are my God; I earnestly search for you. My soul thirsts for you; my whole body longs for you in this parched and weary land where there is no water.   *Psalm 63:1*

I lie in the dust, completely discouraged; revive me by your word.   *Psalm 119:25*

YOUR SOUL IS REFRESHED WHEN YOU thirst after God, seeking him as you would a pool of water in a parched desert. Let him refresh you as you drink in his love for you. Feel your soul revive as you soak in his Word. When you are filled with his love, you will be refreshed.

God's Promise

Satisfy us in the morning with your unfailing love, so we may sing for joy to the end of our lives.   *Psalm 90:14*

Refreshed Mind

In what ways can my mind be refreshed?

God's Response

This is my second letter to you, dear friends, and in both of them I have tried to stimulate your wholesome thinking and refresh your memory. I want you to remember and understand what the holy prophets said long ago and what our Lord and Savior commanded through your apostles.   *2 Peter 3:1-2*

YOUR MIND IS REFRESHED when you read the Bible and allow God's words to calm, encourage, and heal you. Then you will be prepared to let the Holy Spirit change the way you think. Let God's wonderful promises refresh your gratitude as you remember all that he has done for you and refresh your hope as you anticipate all that he promises for the future.

God's Promise

Those who are dominated by the sinful nature think about sinful things, but those who are controlled by the Holy Spirit think about things that please the Spirit. *Romans 8:5*

Refreshed Body

In what ways can my body be refreshed?

God's Response

You have made me as strong as a wild bull. How refreshed I am by your power! *Psalm 92:10*

Moses' arms finally became too tired to hold up the staff any longer. So Aaron and Hur found a stone for him to sit on. Then they stood on each side, holding up his hands until sunset. *Exodus 17:12*

Don't you know that your body is the temple of the Holy Spirit, who lives in you and was given to you by God? You do not belong to yourself, for God bought you with a high price. So you must honor God with your body. *1 Corinthians 6:19-20*

GOD WANTS YOU TO TAKE GOOD CARE of your body, for it is the vehicle for his work in the world. He has given you provisions such as good nourishing food, exercise, sleep, and friends who will help and encourage you when you are weary. Take good care of your body so you can serve the Lord with all your strength.

God's Promise

Fear the LORD and turn your back on evil. Then you will gain renewed health and vitality. *Proverbs 3:7-8*

Refreshing Others

How can I refresh others?

God's Response

May the Lord show special kindness to Onesiphorus and all his family because he often visited and encouraged me. He was never ashamed of me because I was in prison. *2 Timothy 1:16*

I myself have gained much joy and comfort from your love, my brother, because your kindness has so often refreshed the hearts of God's people.   *Philemon 1:7*

The Sovereign LORD has given me his words of wisdom, so that I know what to say to all these weary ones.   *Isaiah 50:4*

YOU CAN REFRESH OTHERS BY being there for them, by acts of kindness large and small, and by carefully chosen words that bring encouragement and joy. Sometimes a smile or a random act of kindness can turn someone's day from bad to beautiful.

God's Promise

A person's words can be life-giving water; words of true wisdom are as refreshing as a bubbling brook. *Proverbs 18:4*

Pleasure

Some people seem to think that pleasure and the Christian life don't mix. Is that true?

God's Response

I decided there is nothing better than to enjoy food and drink and to find satisfaction in work. Then I realized that this pleasure is from the hand of God.   *Ecclesiastes 2:24*

Oh, how delightful you are, my beloved; how pleasant for utter delight!   *Song of Songs 7:6*

The father of godly children has cause for joy. What a pleasure it is to have wise children.   *Proverbs 23:24*

G OD CREATED A BEAUTIFUL WORLD for you to enjoy. He gave you food, drink, and meaningful work to do. Perhaps he has given you a family in which to take pleasure. In fact, he has abundantly given you all things to enjoy. God is pleased when you enjoy the gifts he has given you. This shows him that you appreciate his generosity and kindness.

God's Promise

Since everything God created is good, we should not reject any of it. We may receive it gladly, with thankful hearts. For we know it is made holy by the word of God and prayer.   *1 Timothy 4:4-5*

Pleasing God

In what ways can I give God pleasure?

God's Response

The one who sent me is with me—he has not deserted me. For I always do those things that are pleasing to him. *John 8:29*

It was by faith that Enoch was taken up to heaven without dying. . . . But before he was taken up, he was approved as pleasing to God. So, you see, it is impossible to please God without faith. Anyone who wants to come to him must believe that there is a God and that he rewards those who sincerely seek him. *Hebrews 11:5-6*

WE PLEASE GOD WHEN WE OBEY the instructions found in his Word. God's laws are not designed to burden people or to stifle their fun, but to free them to enjoy life in security and safety. Obeying God protects us from evil that only he knows about, leads us on right paths where we will find blessing, and directs us into service that will please him.

God's Promise

His unchanging plan has always been to adopt us into his own family by bringing us to himself through Jesus Christ. And this gave him great pleasure. *Ephesians 1:5*

Problems

How can I focus on pleasing God when I'm trying to deal with my own problems and obstacles?

God's Response

"Don't worry about a thing," David told Saul. "I'll go fight this Philistine! . . . I have been taking care of my father's sheep. . . . When a lion or a bear comes to steal a lamb from the flock, I go after it with a club. . . . I'll do it to this pagan Philistine, too, for he has defied the armies of the living God! The LORD who saved me from the claws of the lion and the bear will save me from this Philistine!" *1 Samuel 17:32, 34-37*

WHEN YOUR OWN PROBLEMS and obstacles consume you, you will give in to fear—that you will fail, that you will let others down, and that God will not help you when you most need it. Fear will tempt you to focus on the size of the problem rather than on the size of your God. When you focus on God first, you will see him fighting by your side.

God's Promise

You belong to God, my dear children. You have already won your fight with these false prophets, because the Spirit who lives in you is greater than the spirit who lives in the world. *1 John 4:4*

Change

How can I find the courage to face change?

God's Response

LORD, you remain the same forever! Your throne continues from generation to generation.   *Lamentations 5:19*

I am the LORD, and I do not change.   *Malachi 3:6*

God above, who created all heaven's lights . . . never changes or casts shifting shadows. *James 1:17*

SINCE CHANGE IS INEVITABLE in this life, take comfort in the Lord, who never changes. You can rely on his faithfulness, which has not changed from generation to generation; his love, which never shifts or dies; his promises, which are rock solid; and his salvation, which lasts for eternity. When your world spins out of control, cling to the One who controls the universe.

God's Promise

God is not a man, that he should lie. He is not a human, that he should change his mind. Has he ever spoken and failed to act? Has he ever promised and not carried it through? *Numbers 23:19*

Changelessness

With all the change in my life, how can I keep it all together?

God's Response

This change of plans upset Jonah, and he became very angry.   *Jonah 4:1*

You are always the same.   *Hebrews 1:12*

Heaven and earth will disappear, but my words will remain forever.   *Mark 13:31*

CHANGE IS THE ONE THING that never changes. You can be sure that you will always face new challenges. Don't be upset like Jonah when your plans are changed. Instead, build your life on God's Word because its truth is changeless. When you face change, turn to God's Word to maintain your perspective and keep you grounded. Remember the future inheritance that awaits you in heaven, beyond change and decay. That will give you peace.

God's Promise

God has reserved a priceless inheritance for his children. It is kept in heaven for you, pure and undefiled, beyond the reach of change and decay.   *1 Peter 1:4*

Peace Within

How can I find peace within?

God's Response

I will lie down in peace and sleep, for you alone, O LORD, will keep me safe.   *Psalm 4:8*

The LORD gives his people strength. The LORD blesses them with peace.   *Psalm 29:11*

You are my hiding place; you protect me from trouble. You surround me with songs of victory.   *Psalm 32:7*

YOU CAN HAVE INNER PEACE in spite of your circumstances when you fully trust that God is watching over your soul. God's peace does not prevent us from encountering difficulties, but it gives us victory over them. God promises to give us eternal life in a perfect heaven, and he promises that Satan will not steal our souls away from him. When you have total confidence in these two things, then no matter what happens, you can have peace with God.

God's Promise

He who watches over Israel never tires and never sleeps. *Psalm 121:4*

God's Care

With a whole universe to run, how can God watch over me so closely?

God's Response

Not even a sparrow, worth only half a penny, can fall to the ground without your Father knowing it. . . . You are more valuable to him than a whole flock of sparrows. *Matthew 10:29, 31*

I will ask the Father, and he will give you another Counselor, who will never leave you. . . . No, I will not abandon you as orphans—I will come to you. *John 14:16, 18*

GOD WATCHES OVER YOU because he is all-knowing and present everywhere. Jesus also promised that when he ascended to heaven, the Holy Spirit would come and dwell in all believers forever. The almighty God created you, loves you, sustains you, and even knows the number of hairs on your head. If he promises to watch over you, you can trust that he is with you right now.

God's Promise

He will not let you stumble and fall; the one who watches over you will not sleep. Indeed, he who watches over Israel never tires and never sleeps. *Psalm 121:3-4*

God's Promises

How should God's promises change the way I live?

God's Response

Abraham's faith did not weaken, even though he knew that he was too old to be a father at the age of one hundred and that Sarah, his wife, had never been able to have children. Abraham never wavered in believing God's promise. In fact, his faith grew stronger, and in this he brought glory to God. He was absolutely convinced that God was able to do anything he promised.   *Romans 4:19-21*

WHEN YOU ARE CONVINCED that God is able to do anything he promises, then the troubles of this world are put in perspective because you know that your future—for all eternity—is secure. This gives you peace no matter what happens. When you are absolutely convinced that God will keep his promises, you will follow him without hesitation.

God's Promise

God has given us both his promise and his oath. These two things are unchangeable because it is impossible for God to lie. Therefore, we who have fled to him for refuge can take new courage, for we can hold on to his promise with confidence.   *Hebrews 6:18*

Waiting

Why doesn't God fulfill his promises more quickly?
Why must I wait for them to come true?

God's Response

All these faithful ones died without receiving what God had promised them, but they saw it all from a distance and welcomed the promises of God.   *Hebrews 11:13*

MANY GREAT PEOPLE OF GOD have died without seeing God's promises fulfilled, yet they believed that every promise would eventually be realized. Faith in God's promises does not require that you see all his promises fulfilled in your lifetime. Some of God's promises will be fulfilled in heaven, and each of his promises will be fulfilled in his perfect timing, when it will accomplish the greatest good. Your waiting is never in vain because it makes you strong and confident for the future.

God's Promise

You must remain faithful to what you have been taught from the beginning. If you do, you will continue to live in fellowship with the Son and with the Father. And in this fellowship we enjoy the eternal life he promised us.
1 John 2:24-25

A Stronger Faith

How can waiting make my faith stronger?

God's Response

The LORD your God will drive those nations out ahead of you little by little. You will not clear them away all at once, for if you did, the wild animals would multiply too quickly for you.   *Deuteronomy 7:22*

Oh, there is so much more I want to tell you, but you can't bear it now.   *John 16:12*

When the right time came, God sent his Son.   *Galatians 4:4*

GOD OFTEN ASKS YOU TO wait while leading you along the path of progressive, not immediate, victory. Why? Sometimes this keeps you from the pride that often comes after success. Sometimes it saves you from defeat. And sometimes God makes you wait to prepare you for a special work he has for you. Waiting is never time wasted by God, so don't waste it by being anxious. Serve God as you wait for him to accomplish the next good thing in your life.

God's Challenge

Be still in the presence of the LORD, and wait patiently for him to act. Don't worry about evil people who prosper or fret about their wicked schemes.   *Psalm 37:7*

Waiting

How should I respond in a time of waiting?

God's Response

The Kingdom of Heaven can be illustrated by the story of a man going on a trip. He called together his servants and gave them money to invest for him while he was gone. He gave five bags of gold to one. . . . After a long time their master returned from his trip and called them to give an account of how they had used his money. The servant to whom he had entrusted the five bags of gold said, "Sir, you gave me five bags of gold to invest, and I have doubled the amount." The master was full of praise. *Matthew 25:14-15, 19-21*

AS YOU WAIT, SERVE. The servant in the parable was praised for working diligently and intelligently while the master was gone, and you can be confident that Jesus wants you to faithfully and wisely serve him right where you are as you await your next instructions.

God's Promise

Well done, my good and faithful servant. You have been faithful in handling this small amount, so now I will give you many more responsibilities. Let's celebrate together! *Matthew 25:21*

Confidence

Why should I be confident in God?

God's Response

The LORD is my light and my salvation—so why should I be afraid? The LORD protects me from danger—so why should I tremble?   *Psalm 27:1*

Does your reverence for God give you no confidence? Shouldn't you believe that God will care for those who are upright?   *Job 4:6*

My heart is confident in you, O God; no wonder I can sing your praises!   *Psalm 57:7*

OUR CONFIDENCE IN GOD is often misguided. We think that our faith would be stronger if he gave us things that made our lives easier and more comfortable, but we're not setting our sights high enough. The things we want often distract us from the God we long for.

God's Promise

Oh, the joys of those who trust the LORD, who have no confidence in the proud, or in those who worship idols. *Psalm 40:4*

Faith

I know I'm supposed to have faith in God, but it seems so complicated. How can I ever have faith?

God's Response

Jesus prayed this prayer: "O Father, Lord of heaven and earth, thank you for hiding the truth from those who think themselves so wise and clever, and for revealing it to the childlike." *Matthew 11:25*

W E OFTEN MAKE FAITH IN GOD more complicated than it really is. Faith simply means trusting God to do what he has promised. The problem comes when we get confused over exactly what he has promised. Studying God's promises in the Bible is a great use of your time. Then you will develop a childlike confidence in God as you see all the promises he has fulfilled and anticipate the ones yet to come.

God's Promise

He said to Thomas, "Put your finger here and see my hands. Put your hand into the wound in my side. Don't be faithless any longer. Believe!"

"My Lord and my God!" Thomas exclaimed.

Then Jesus told him, "You believe because you have seen me. Blessed are those who haven't seen me and believe anyway." *John 20:27-29*

Exercise

How can I strengthen my faith?

God's Response

I honor and love your commands. I meditate on your principles. . . . Your principles have been the music of my life throughout the years of my pilgrimage. *Psalm 119:48, 54*

Faith comes from listening to this message of good news— the Good News about Christ. *Romans 10:17*

The LORD told Abram, "Leave your country." . . . So Abram departed as the LORD had instructed him. *Genesis 12:1, 4*

L IKE A MUSCLE, faith gets stronger as you exercise it. When you rely on God during hard times and see him come through for you, your faith grows stronger for your next trial or test. Spend time in the "gym" of God's Word, building your muscles of faith and toning up on his promises and faithful character.

God's Promise

If your faith remains strong after being tried by fiery trials, it will bring you much praise and glory and honor on the day when Jesus Christ is revealed to the whole world. *1 Peter 1:7*

Tiny Faith

How much faith must I have?

God's Response

Jesus told them, "I assure you, even if you had faith as small as a mustard seed you could say to this mountain, 'Move from here to there,' and it would move. Nothing would be impossible."   *Matthew 17:20*

THE MUSTARD SEED WAS the smallest seed known to exist in Bible times. It is used to illustrate faith because a huge plant grew from this tiny seed. Likewise, just a tiny bit of faith in Jesus may be planted in your soul, but over time, faith will grow big enough to move mountains of trouble and doubt. Jesus says that it is not the size of your faith but the size of the One in whom you believe that makes the difference. You do not have to have great faith in God; rather you have faith in a great God. So give God even your little bits of faith, and he will do the rest.

God's Promise

Take courage! For I believe God. It will be just as he said.
Acts 27:25

Lifeline

How does faith in God affect my life?

God's Response

Abram believed the LORD, and the LORD declared him righteous because of his faith.   *Genesis 15:6*

God in his gracious kindness declares us not guilty. . . . We are made right with God when we believe that Jesus shed his blood, sacrificing his life for us.   *Romans 3:24-25*

FAITH IS YOUR LIFELINE TO GOD. Sin breaks your relationship with God because it is rebellion against him. When you accept Jesus as your Savior and ask him to forgive your sins, this simple act of faith makes you righteous in God's sight. In other words, God looks at you as though you have never sinned. You can live free from guilt and confident of eternal life.

God's Promise

God, in his mighty power, will protect you until you receive this salvation, because you are trusting him. It will be revealed on the last day for all to see.
1 Peter 1:5

Doubts

When I'm struggling in my Christian life and have doubts, does it mean that I have less faith?

God's Response

John the Baptist . . . sent his disciples to ask Jesus, "Are you really the Messiah we've been waiting for?" *Matthew 11:2-3*

He climbed into the boat, and the wind stopped. They were astonished at what they saw. They still didn't understand the significance of the miracle of the multiplied loaves, for their hearts were hard and they did not believe. *Mark 6:51-52*

MANY PEOPLE THAT WE READ about in the Bible had moments of doubt. Doubts are valuable when they bring you closer to God. When you doubt, don't be afraid to ask questions. God can handle your doubts, so tell him what's on your mind, and expect him to respond. Doubt is human. The church would be a lot healthier—and more attractive to unbelievers—if Christians stopped pretending that they never doubted.

God's Promise

He has given us all of his rich and wonderful promises. . . . So make every effort to apply the benefits of these promises to your life. *2 Peter 1:4-5*

Doubts

When I face doubts, it's hard to keep going.
How can I persevere in those times?

God's Response

I am willing to endure anything if it will bring salvation and eternal glory in Christ Jesus to those God has chosen. This is a true saying: "If we die with him, we will also live with him. If we endure hardship, we will reign with him. If we deny him, he will deny us." *2 Timothy 2:10-12*

Patient endurance is what you need now, so you will continue to do God's will. Then you will receive all that he has promised. *Hebrews 10:36*

W HEN YOU BEGIN TO DOUBT and troubles come your way that cause you to ask if what you believe is really true, you need to just be obedient during this time of testing. What makes doubt spiritually healthy or unhealthy is what you do with it. You can allow doubt to debilitate your faith or you can let it carry you to God. Bring your questions to God, and he will turn them into faith.

God's Promise

When doubts filled my mind, your comfort gave me renewed hope and cheer. *Psalm 94:19*

Commitment

Why is it so important to stay committed to Jesus—through the doubts and through the tough times?

God's Response

Complete the ministry God has given you. . . . I have fought a good fight, I have finished the race, and I have remained faithful. And now the prize awaits me—the crown of righteousness that the Lord, the righteous Judge, will give me on that great day of his return. And the prize is not just for me but for all who eagerly look forward to his glorious return.   *2 Timothy 4:5, 7-8*

GOD'S PROMISE IS SURE, and you must always keep your eyes on that. God never promised that life on earth would be easy, but he does promise to walk with you every step of the way and bring you into glory when he returns. Stay committed to Christ as he is committed to you. Keep serving him in whatever ways he asks. In the end, your obedience will be rewarded, and your reward will be beyond all expectation.

God's Promise

All who are victorious will be clothed in white. I will never erase their names from the Book of Life.   *Revelation 3:5*

Hospitality

How can I show hospitality to others?

God's Response

Cheerfully share your home with those who need a meal or a place to stay. *1 Peter 4:9*

"My lords," he said, "come to my home to wash your feet, and be my guests for the night. You may then get up in the morning as early as you like and be on your way again." *Genesis 19:2*

The man went home with Laban, and Laban unloaded the camels, gave him straw to bed them down, fed them, and provided water for the camel drivers to wash their feet. *Genesis 24:32*

THE BASICS OF GOOD HOSPITALITY—a place to stay and food to eat—are simple acts of kindness that you can offer to anyone. Being hospitable is a way to obey and serve God, because God calls us to love and serve others as though we were serving him. When we care for the physical needs of others, we are serving Jesus as if he were our guest.

God's Promise

Don't forget to show hospitality to strangers, for some who have done this have entertained angels without realizing it! *Hebrews 13:2*

Hospitality

My home is nothing special, and I'm not a great cook. How can I be hospitable?

God's Response

You are doing a good work for God when you take care of the traveling teachers who are passing through.   *3 John 1:5*

Her sister, Mary, sat at the Lord's feet, listening to what he taught. . . . "There is really only one thing worth being concerned about. Mary has discovered it—and I won't take it away from her." *Luke 10:39, 42*

DON'T FALL INTO THE TRAP of thinking that you must have a big house or extraordinary culinary skills in order to be hospitable. Instead of making your home and food your focus, make your guests the focus. The most important part of hospitality is ministering to the needs of others and sharing the Lord's blessings with them. The surroundings then become insignificant.

God's Promise

I was hungry, and you fed me. I was thirsty, and you gave me a drink. I was a stranger, and you invited me into your home. . . . And the King will tell them, "I assure you, when you did it to one of the least of these my brothers and sisters, you were doing it to me!" *Matthew 25:35, 40*

Friendship

How can I be a good friend?

God's Response

Jonathan made David reaffirm his vow of friendship.
1 Samuel 20:17

A friend is always loyal, and a brother is born to help in time of need.   *Proverbs 17:17*

The godly give good advice to their friends; the wicked lead them astray.   *Proverbs 12:26*

Wounds from a friend are better than many kisses from an enemy.   *Proverbs 27:6*

As iron sharpens iron, a friend sharpens a friend.
Proverbs 27:17

TRUE FRIENDSHIPS ARE GLUED together by bonds of loyalty and commitment. They remain intact despite changing external circumstances. True friends show love and kindness and are able to be honest with each other. It is even better when true friends share a common commitment to Jesus.

God's Promise

Where two or three gather together because they are mine, I am there among them.   *Matthew 18:20*

Outsider

How can I make friends when I feel like an outsider?

God's Response

Dear brothers and sisters, you are foreigners and aliens here. So I warn you to keep away from evil desires because they fight against your very souls.   *1 Peter 2:11*

God blesses you who are hated and excluded and mocked and cursed because you are identified with me, the Son of Man.   *Luke 6:22*

I am but a foreigner here on earth; I need the guidance of your commands. Don't hide them from me! *Psalm 119:19*

IN SOME CASES, you may feel like an outsider because of your faith. Don't compromise your beliefs in order to have friends; instead, ask God to guide you to other believers with whom you can find fellowship and to non-believers who are seeking faith. Realize that feeling like an outsider is natural, for your true home is in heaven.

God's Promise

They agreed that they were no more than foreigners and nomads here on earth. . . . But they were looking for a better place, a heavenly homeland.   *Hebrews 11:13, 16*

Empathy

How can I show sensitivity to those who appear to be on the outside looking in?

God's Response

Do not oppress foreigners in any way. Remember, you yourselves were once foreigners in the land of Egypt. *Exodus 22:21*

I want you to share your food with the hungry and to welcome poor wanderers into your homes. Give clothes to those who need them, and do not hide from relatives who need your help.   *Isaiah 58:7*

THINK ABOUT A TIME WHEN you were an outsider. How did you feel? What would have helped you? When you can empathize with others, you will know how to help them feel welcome. Look around today and notice someone who looks lonely. Greet them with a cheerful smile. Who knows? You may be greeting a wonderful new friend!

God's Challenge

This is what the LORD Almighty says: Judge fairly and honestly, and show mercy and kindness to one another. Do not oppress widows, orphans, foreigners, and poor people. And do not make evil plans to harm each other. *Zechariah 7:9-10*

Government

How should I pray for my country?

God's Response

Pray this way for kings and all others who are in authority, so that we can live in peace and quietness, in godliness and dignity.   *1 Timothy 2:2*

When there is moral rot within a nation, its government topples easily.   *Proverbs 28:2*

PRAY THAT YOUR NATION will be protected by God's mighty hand. Pray that your leaders will be humble and wise, able to discern right from wrong and to champion the needy and helpless. A nation that endorses and condones immorality is subject to judgment and will eventually collapse from the inside out. A nation that walks in the ways of the Lord will stand firm.

God's Promise

If my people who are called by my name will humble themselves and pray and seek my face and turn from their wicked ways, I will hear from heaven and will forgive their sins and heal their land.   *2 Chronicles 7:14*

Freedom

What does it mean to be free in Christ?

God's Response

You are not slaves; you are free. But your freedom is not an excuse to do evil. You are free to live as God's slaves. *1 Peter 2:16*

Christ has really set us free. Now make sure that you stay free, and don't get tied up again in slavery to the law. *Galatians 5:1*

The Lord is the Spirit, and wherever the Spirit of the Lord is, he gives freedom. *2 Corinthians 3:17*

FREEDOM IN CHRIST MEANS freedom from all the things in life that bring you down—guilt, sin, fear, addiction. This does not operate in a vacuum; you are free to do many other things—free to follow Christ, free to let go of self and worship God, free to live by the truth of God's Word, and free to serve him wholeheartedly.

God's Promise

You will know the truth, and the truth will set you free. . . . So if the Son sets you free, you will indeed be free. *John 8:32, 36*

Celebration

I want to celebrate Jesus! How can I do that?

God's Response

Sing for joy, O heavens! Rejoice, O earth! Burst into song, O mountains!   *Isaiah 49:13*

This day in early spring will be the anniversary of your exodus. You must celebrate this day. . . . During these festival days each year, you must explain to your children why you are celebrating.   *Exodus 13:4-5, 8*

Many sacrifices were offered on that joyous day, for God had given the people cause for great joy. . . . The joy of the people of Jerusalem could be heard far away. *Nehemiah 12:43*

YOU CAN CELEBRATE BY USING YOUR VOICE. Sing, praise, rejoice, and share what Jesus has done for you. All celebration should glorify God with the joy that comes from a full and grateful heart. Those who love him truly have the most to celebrate!

God's Promise

This festival will be a happy time of rejoicing with your family . . . to honor the LORD . . . for it is [he] who gives you bountiful harvests and blesses all your work. *Deuteronomy 16:14-15*

Enthusiasm

Is it okay to celebrate my faith? I thought it was all so serious.

God's Response

In fact, it was your enthusiasm that stirred up many of them to begin helping. *2 Corinthians 9:2*

Work hard and cheerfully at whatever you do, as though you were working for the Lord rather than for people. *Colossians 3:23*

Rejoice in the LORD and be glad, all you who obey him! Shout for joy, all you whose hearts are pure! *Psalm 32:11*

THE DECISION TO FOLLOW CHRIST is serious, but the Christian life should be full of delight and joy. In fact, God's Word tells you to serve him enthusiastically, to sing, dance, play music, and set aside special days of joy, food, and fellowship. Serve God with enthusiasm and your joy will be infectious.

God's Promise

Praise the LORD, I tell myself, and never forget the good things he does for me. *Psalm 103:2*

Shallow Faith

*What can dampen my enthusiasm for Jesus,
and how can I guard against that?*

God's Response

The rocky soil represents those who hear the message and receive it with joy. But like young plants in such soil, their roots don't go very deep. At first they get along fine, but they wilt as soon as they have problems or are persecuted. *Matthew 13:20-21*

You must warn each other every day, as long as it is called "today," so that none of you will be deceived by sin and hardened against God. *Hebrews 3:13*

WHEN YOU GET SERIOUS ABOUT YOUR FAITH, your enthusiasm for God grows by leaps and bounds. To prevent your faith from becoming shallow when you face problems, read God's Word daily, study it, refuse to be deceived by sin, and learn how Satan tries to tempt you. Keep your focus on being a representative of Jesus Christ. God promises you more joy than you have ever thought possible.

God's Promise

When you obey me . . . you will be filled with my joy. Yes, your joy will overflow! *John 15:10-11*

Availability

How can I let God know that I'm available for him to use?

God's Response

Later on God tested Abraham's faith and obedience. "Abraham!" God called.

"Yes," he replied. "Here I am."   *Genesis 22:1*

I heard the Lord asking, "Whom should I send as a messenger to my people? Who will go for us?"

And I said, "Lord, I'll go! Send me."   *Isaiah 6:8*

PERFECTION IS NOT A REQUIREMENT for God to use you. Your obedient response to God's call is enough; it shows that you are available to him. You should be eager to obey whatever God calls you to do. When your heart pounds and your hands sweat when you hear of opportunities to serve, you can be sure that the Holy Spirit is urging you to respond. Go for it, and be ready to be used and blessed by God in a wonderful way.

God's Promise

If you keep yourself pure, you will be a utensil God can use for his purpose. Your life will be clean, and you will be ready for the Master to use you for every good work. *2 Timothy 2:21*

Surrender

What does it mean to "surrender my life" to God?

God's Response

LORD, you are our Father. We are the clay, and you are the potter. We are all formed by your hand.   *Isaiah 64:8*

He called his disciples and the crowds to come over and listen. "If any of you wants to be my follower," he told them, "you must put aside your selfish ambition, shoulder your cross, and follow me."   *Mark 8:34*

I myself no longer live, but Christ lives in me. So I live my life in this earthly body by trusting in the Son of God, who loved me and gave himself for me.   *Galatians 2:20*

WHEN YOU SURRENDER TO GOD, you give up what you think is best for your life and do what he knows is best. You put aside your self-fulfilling ambitions so that you can do the job Jesus has for you. You ask Jesus, through the power of the Holy Spirit, to live in you and through you. You give up the control of your life to almighty God, who created you, loves you, knows you, and has a plan for you.

God's Promise

You died when Christ died, and your real life is hidden with Christ in God.   *Colossians 3:3*

Surrender

How do I surrender my life to God?

God's Response

May your Kingdom come soon. May your will be done here on earth, just as it is in heaven.   *Matthew 6:10*

What you ought to say is, "If the Lord wants us to, we will live and do this or that."   *James 4:15*

This world is fading away, along with everything it craves. But if you do the will of God, you will live forever. *1 John 2:17*

TO SURRENDER YOUR LIFE TO GOD, you must put his will above your own. God's will is simply what God wants for you, and this is clearly written in the Bible. Consider everything you plan or do through the filter of the Scriptures. Do your intentions contradict what God says in his Word? Is it right or wrong? Does it serve others or self? Consider your plans through prayer. Do you feel at peace about them when talking to God? When you seek God first in all things, your life will be surrendered to him.

God's Promise

He will give you all you need from day to day if you live for him and make the Kingdom of God your primary concern.   *Matthew 6:33*

Abundance

What is the abundance that God wants me to experience?

God's Response

May you experience the love of Christ, though it is so great you will never fully understand it. Then you will be filled with the fullness of life and power that comes from God.   *Ephesians 3:19*

You feed them from the abundance of your own house, letting them drink from your rivers of delight.   *Psalm 36:8*

TOO OFTEN WE DEFINE ABUNDANCE quantitatively by how many possessions or how much financial wealth we have. Instead, we should think of abundance as God does—the marvelous gift of salvation and eternal life; the blessing of a relationship with the Creator of the universe; the treasure of God's Word; and the wonderful character traits of godliness, truth, wisdom, and a good reputation. These riches are lasting and priceless, and this abundance is guaranteed by our obedience.

God's Promise

If you give, you will receive. Your gift will return to you in full measure, pressed down, shaken together to make room for more, and running over.   *Luke 6:38*

Satisfaction

How does God's abundance satisfy the longings in my life?

God's Response

If you only knew the gift God has for you and who I am, you would ask me, and I would give you living water. . . . People soon become thirsty again after drinking this water. But the water I give them takes away thirst altogether. It becomes a perpetual spring within them, giving them eternal life. *John 4:10, 13-14*

Jesus replied, "I am the bread of life. No one who comes to me will ever be hungry again. Those who believe in me will never thirst." *John 6:35*

I T'S A PRINCIPLE AS OLD AS CREATION that having more things does not bring great personal satisfaction. Only the Lord can fulfill your deepest longings, because he built them into you from the moment he made you. When you learn how a relationship with him truly satisfies, you will stop longing for things that can never satisfy.

God's Promise

He satisfies the thirsty and fills the hungry with good things. *Psalm 107:9*

Happiness

Will God give me real, lasting happiness?

God's Response

O LORD Almighty, happy are those who trust in you.
Psalm 84:12

Happy are those who obey his decrees and search for him
with all their hearts.   *Psalm 119:2*

Happy are those who fear the LORD. Yes, happy are those
who delight in doing what he commands.   *Psalm 112:1*

WE ARE HAPPY WHEN A TOOL—a whisk, kitchen
knife, or garden clipper—works in the way it was
intended to. This feeling of happiness is just a shadow of
the lasting happiness we will experience when, as human
beings, we function in the way God intended when he
made us. He made us to live and relate to others in certain ways that are clearly described in the Bible. When
we function as God intended, we discover real, lasting
happiness, and we have the greatest possible impact on
our present and our future. Achieving our purpose brings
true happiness.

God's Promise

The godly can look forward to happiness.   *Proverbs 11:23*

Service

How can I bring happiness to others?

God's Response

Love each other with genuine affection, and take delight in honoring each other.   *Romans 12:10*

In addition to our own encouragement, we were especially delighted to see how happy Titus was at the way you welcomed him and set his mind at ease.   *2 Corinthians 7:13*

WHILE WE CANNOT MAKE another person totally happy, we can bring a bit of delight into their day. By taking a few moments to write a note of encouragement, call to check on them, run an errand, or do a favor, we can brighten someone's life by showing that we care. Whether we are sharing an amusing moment, celebrating a happy event, shouldering a burden, or shedding tears of mutual sorrow, people know we care when we spend time with them. Time spent in serving and loving others is never wasted, and it brings much happiness to both the receiver and the giver.

God's Promise

Dear friends, let us continue to love one another, for love comes from God. Anyone who loves is born of God and knows God.   *1 John 4:7*

God's Happiness

How can I bring God happiness?

God's Response

The LORD your God will delight in you if you obey his voice and keep the commands and laws written in this Book of the Law, and if you turn to the LORD your God with all your heart and soul.   *Deuteronomy 30:10*

The LORD . . . delights in honesty . . . in those who have integrity.   *Proverbs 11:1, 20*

The LORD . . . delights in the prayers of the upright.   *Proverbs 15:8*

The LORD . . . delights in pure words.   *Proverbs 15:26*

L IKE A FATHER WITH HIS CHILD, God is delighted when we love him with all our heart and soul. He loves it when we imitate his character with integrity, honesty, and purity of heart. When you obey God, it shows him that you love him enough to trust him with your life.

God's Promise

The LORD your God has arrived to live among you. He is a mighty savior. He will rejoice over you with great gladness. With his love, he will calm all your fears. He will exult over you by singing a happy song.   *Zephaniah 3:17*

Joy

Is it possible to be happy in the middle of difficult circumstances?

God's Response

Dear friends, don't be surprised at the fiery trials you are going through, as if something strange were happening to you. Instead, be very glad . . . you will have the wonderful joy of sharing his glory.   *1 Peter 4:12-13*

I T MAY NOT ALWAYS BE POSSIBLE to be happy, but it is always possible to have joy. Happiness is temporary because it is based on external circumstances; true joy is lasting because it is based on God's constant presence and comfort. If you base your happiness on circumstances, there will be many times when you will not be happy; but when you trust God with your life, you will begin to understand that your troubles are part of an epic story that has the happy ending of eternity in paradise with God. This knowledge will help you to have joy even in the worst of circumstances.

God's Promise

When you go through deep waters and great trouble, I will be with you. When you go through rivers of difficulty, you will not drown! When you walk through the fire of oppression, you will not be burned up; the flames will not consume you.   *Isaiah 43:2*

Challenges

Why does God let me face so many challenges?

God's Response

Be strong and very courageous. Obey all the laws Moses gave you. Do not turn away from them, and you will be successful in everything you do.   *Joshua 1:7*

Dear brothers and sisters, whenever trouble comes your way, let it be an opportunity for joy. For when your faith is tested, your endurance has a chance to grow. So let it grow, for when your endurance is fully developed, you will be strong in character and ready for anything.   *James 1:2-4*

CHALLENGES THAT THREATEN or overwhelm you are the very tools God uses to bring you to greater strength and maturity. He sends some challenges into your life; others, he merely allows. As you endure these times, you develop greater wisdom, integrity, and courage to face whatever comes your way. We usually most value those things that we have worked the hardest to attain.

God's Promise

In your strength I can crush an army; with my God I can scale any wall.   *2 Samuel 22:30*

Challenges

How should challenges shape my life?

God's Response

Afterward Paul felt impelled by the Holy Spirit to go over to Macedonia and Achaia before returning to Jerusalem. "And after that," he said, "I must go on to Rome!"   *Acts 19:21*

I want you to know, dear brothers and sisters, that everything that has happened to me here has helped to spread the Good News. For everyone here, including all the soldiers in the palace guard, knows that I am in chains because of Christ.   *Philippians 1:12-13*

C HALLENGES KEEP YOU FROM being comfortable and satisfied with the status quo, and force you to follow God's leading into uncharted waters. Paul's vision to preach the gospel continually drove him to new challenges. He even saw his time in prison as an opportunity to witness to the soldiers who guarded him! View your challenges as occasions for spiritual growth.

God's Promise

Be strong and take courage, all you who put your hope in the LORD!   *Psalm 31:24*

Risks

What kinds of risks should I take?

God's Response

When you work in a quarry, stones might fall and crush you! When you chop wood, there is danger with each stroke of your ax! Such are the risks of life. *Ecclesiastes 10:9*

A prudent person foresees the danger ahead and takes precautions; the simpleton goes blindly on and suffers the consequences. *Proverbs 22:3*

Do not be afraid of the terrors of the night, nor fear the dangers of the day. *Psalm 91:5*

GROWTH AND SUCCESS OCCUR at some risk. Taking foolish chances is not risk, but stupidity. Risk entails a good goal, a decent chance of achieving it, and a strong dose of trust. Risk is actually necessary if we want to grow in our relationship with God. When he calls you to do something out of your comfort zone, obey at the risk of failing, while trusting him to help you complete what he has asked you to do.

God's Promise

Commit everything you do to the LORD. Trust him, and he will help you. *Psalm 37:5*

Opportunity

How do I make the most of the opportunities that come my way?

God's Response

Make the most of every opportunity for doing good in these evil days.   *Ephesians 5:16*

Hard work means prosperity; only fools idle away their time.   *Proverbs 12:11*

In the meantime, I will be staying here at Ephesus . . . for there is a wide-open door for a great work here, and many people are responding.   *1 Corinthians 16:8-9*

WHEN YOU BELIEVE THAT GOD is presenting you with an opportunity, respond quickly and work hard to maximize what God has put before you. Be willing to change your plans in order to take advantage of any God-given opportunity. You will be motivated when you think of how God might use you because you've made yourself available for his work. Keep your eyes open for what God will bring your way.

God's Challenge

All of us must quickly carry out the tasks assigned us by the one who sent me, because there is little time left before the night falls and all work comes to an end.   *John 9:4*

Opportunity

How do I know if an opportunity is from God?

God's Response

Philip ran over and heard the man reading from the prophet Isaiah; so he asked, "Do you understand what you are reading?" *Acts 8:30*

Keep on praying. *1 Thessalonians 5:17*

The LORD said to Moses, "Why are you crying out to me? Tell the people to get moving!" *Exodus 14:15*

A NY OPPORTUNITY THAT CONTRADICTS God's Word or violates its principles is not from the Lord. You have to read the Bible if you want to know what it says. The Bible may not directly address a particular opportunity, but it gives clear guidelines about what you should and should not do. The more you know the Bible, the more you know the mind of God, and therefore the better you can discern whether the next opportunity is something he wants you to act on. Once you know it is from God, get moving!

God's Promise

Your word is a lamp for my feet and a light for my path. *Psalm 119:105*

Discernment

Where should I turn for direction when I'm not sure which path to take?

God's Response

If you need wisdom—if you want to know what God wants you to do—ask him, and he will gladly tell you. He will not resent your asking. But when you ask him, be sure that you really expect him to answer. *James 1:5-6*

Give discernment to me, your servant; then I will understand your decrees. *Psalm 119:125*

DISCERNMENT IS THE ABILITY to interpret events and know what is of God and what takes us away from God. It helps us to decide what must be done, and to understand people's true motives. Discernment separates right from wrong, good from bad, helpful from harmful. The best way for you to discern whether something is from God is to know what God has called you to. Anything that does not take you in that direction is the wrong way for you, even if it is something that is okay in itself.

God's Promise

If you live a life guided by wisdom, you won't limp or stumble as you run. *Proverbs 4:12*

Discernment

*In what other areas of my life do I need
to be discerning?*

God's Response

"Just as the mouth tastes good food, the ear tests the words
it hears." So let us discern for ourselves what is right; let us
learn together what is good.   *Job 34:3-4*

The godly give good advice, but fools are destroyed by
their lack of common sense.   *Proverbs 10:21*

I know full well that false teachers, like vicious wolves, will
come in among you after I leave, not sparing the flock.
Even some of you will distort the truth in order to draw
a following. Watch out!   *Acts 20:29-31*

TO DEVELOP DISCERNMENT BETWEEN right and wrong,
between good advice and bad advice, and between
true and false teachings, you must immerse yourself in
God's Word and then pay attention to how God deals
with you personally. Discernment in these three areas will
give you the foundation for a godly life.

God's Promise

Getting wisdom is the most important thing you can
do! And whatever else you do, get good judgment.
Proverbs 4:7

God's Will

How do I know what God wants me to do?

God's Response

Coming to the borders of Mysia, they headed for the province of Bithynia, but again the Spirit of Jesus did not let them go. So instead, they went on through Mysia to the city of Troas. That night Paul had a vision. He saw a man from Macedonia in northern Greece, pleading with him, "Come over here and help us." So we decided to leave for Macedonia at once, for we could only conclude that God was calling us to preach the Good News there.   *Acts 16:7-10*

GOD'S WILL IS BOTH GENERAL AND SPECIFIC. God's general will is for all people and is found in the Bible. It includes things that God expects from everyone, such as obedience, service, worship, fellowship, and prayer. God's specific will is his plan for you as an individual. It may include your job, marriage partner, or a unique task he wants you to accomplish. When you follow God's general will, you are exactly where he wants you, fully prepared to step into his specific will when he calls. You will hear him.

God's Promise

You chart the path ahead of me and tell me where to stop and rest. Every moment you know where I am.
Psalm 139:3

Values

How do my values affect my choices?

God's Response

"Come and sleep with me," she demanded.

But Joseph refused. "Look," he told her, "my master trusts me with everything in his entire household. . . . How could I do such a wicked thing? It would be a great sin against God."   *Genesis 39:7-9 (NLT2)*

Do for others what you would like them to do for you. This is a summary of all that is taught in the law.   *Matthew 7:12*

I T'S EASY TO SEE WHAT YOU REALLY VALUE by the choices you make. Just consider how you spend your money and your time, what you think most about, and what arouses the passions of your heart. Then ask yourself this question: How do I view acts that the Bible calls sin, such as white lies or ignoring wrongdoing, gossip, flattery, profanity, or cheating? If you don't see these as sin, you must face the fact that your values differ from the Bible's, and your choices will not be pleasing to God.

God's Challenge

Obscene stories, foolish talk, and coarse jokes—these are not for you. Instead, let there be thankfulness to God.
Ephesians 5:4

Behavior

How should my choices affect my behavior?

God's Response

We are instructed to turn from godless living and sinful pleasures. We should live in this evil world with self-control, right conduct, and devotion to God.   *Titus 2:12*

You should behave . . . like God's very own children. *Romans 8:15*

Let your good deeds shine out for all to see, so that everyone will praise your heavenly Father.   *Matthew 5:16*

YOUR VALUES AFFECT YOUR CHOICES, and your choices affect your behavior. Your behavior reveals your heart, or what is most important to you. When you claim to be a follower of God, make sure that others can truly see you following him. Then many will want to follow as well because they will like what they see.

God's Promise

Even more blessed are all who hear the word of God and put it into practice.   *Luke 11:28*

Example

How am I supposed to live as a believer?

God's Response

Be an example to all believers in what you teach, in the way you live, in your love, your faith, and your purity.
1 Timothy 4:12

When Abram was ninety-nine years old, the LORD appeared to him and said, "I am God Almighty; serve me faithfully and live a blameless life."   *Genesis 17:1*

GOD GAVE ABRAM TWO CLEAR GOALS for living that apply to us as well: Serve God faithfully and live a blameless life. Both of these goals have a lot to do with our motives. God knows that we are sinners (the Bible points out several of Abram's sins). But if, as believers, our heart's desire is to faithfully obey God and avoid sin to the best of our ability, God will be pleased.

God's Challenge

Don't copy the behavior and customs of this world, but let God transform you into a new person by changing the way you think.   *Romans 12:2*

Righteousness

How can I be righteous before God?

God's Response

Since we have been made right in God's sight by faith, we have peace with God because of what Jesus Christ our Lord has done for us. Because of our faith, Christ has brought us into this place of highest privilege where we now stand, and we confidently and joyfully look forward to sharing God's glory.   *Romans 5:1-2*

God made Christ, who never sinned, to be the offering for our sin, so that we could be made right with God through Christ.   *2 Corinthians 5:21*

GOD DOES NOT REGARD YOU AS righteous because you are sinless, but because Jesus died to take your sins away. No one but Jesus Christ lived a sinless life, but a person who acknowledges Jesus as Lord sincerely tries to live in obedience to God's Word. Anyone who seeks forgiveness for sin can be called righteous. In other words, God looks at you as though you have not sinned.

God's Promise

This Good News tells us how God makes us right in his sight. This is accomplished from start to finish by faith. *Romans 1:17*

Righteousness

How can I pursue and practice righteousness?

God's Response

Run from all these evil things, and follow what is right and good. Pursue a godly life, along with faith, love, perseverance, and gentleness.   *1 Timothy 6:11*

"Lord, when did we ever see you hungry . . . or thirsty . . . or a stranger . . . sick or in prison?" And the King will tell them, "I assure you, when you did it to one of the least of these my brothers and sisters, you were doing it to me!" *Matthew 25:37-40*

PURSUING AND PRACTICING RIGHTEOUSNESS is a three-part process. First, you have to run from evil, that is, turn your back on anything that is wrong, deceitful, and immoral. Then you have to run after that which is good and right, such as faith, love, perseverance, and gentleness. Finally, you have to put your righteousness into practice by helping those in need. The pursuit and practice of righteousness is proactive, not just idle theory.

God's Promise

Whoever pursues godliness and unfailing love will find life, godliness, and honor.   *Proverbs 21:21*

God's Power

In what ways does God's power help me to be more like Christ?

God's Response

A final word: Be strong with the Lord's mighty power. Put on all of God's armor so that you will be able to stand firm against all strategies and tricks of the Devil. For we are not fighting against people made of flesh and blood, but against the evil rulers and authorities of the unseen world, against those mighty powers of darkness who rule this world, and against wicked spirits in the heavenly realms. *Ephesians 6:10-12*

IT IS NOT ENOUGH TO MERELY IMITATE Christ by trying through your own efforts to do right and seek God's will. Instead, you are indwelt by the Holy Spirit, and his power works through you. You thus equip yourself for battle against Satan and his evil army. You will need to work hard and use all of God's power in you to stand firm, but the Holy Spirit's power is much greater than Satan's, and you can win the battle.

God's Promise

The Spirit who lives in you is greater than the spirit who lives in the world.   *1 John 4:4*

Comparisons

What are the standards against which I should compare myself?

God's Response

As the Spirit of the Lord works within us, we become more and more like him and reflect his glory even more.
2 Corinthians 3:18

I T'S NOT REALLY HELPFUL to compare yourself to other people, because God created each person as a unique individual with their own gifts and talents. Jesus is the ultimate standard of a good person. No one can fully measure up to Jesus because he is perfect, but you can try to be as much like him as possible. When you give up everything to be like Jesus, you are consumed with being godly, which will lead you into doing what is good and right. Don't compare yourself with other people—concentrate on being the best Christian you can be.

God's Promise

Just as we are now like Adam, the man of the earth, so we will someday be like Christ, the man from heaven.
1 Corinthians 15:49

Comparisons

What are the dangers of comparing myself with others?

God's Response

This was their song: "Saul has killed his thousands, and David his ten thousands!" This made Saul very angry. *1 Samuel 18:7-8*

We want to be like the nations around us.   *1 Samuel 8:20*

The proud Pharisee stood by himself and prayed this prayer: "I thank you, God, that I am not a sinner like everyone else, especially like that tax collector over there!"   *Luke 18:11*

WHEN YOU COMPARE YOURSELF to others, you take your eyes off of Jesus, which will cause you problems. You may want what others have, and become jealous and discontented. You may want to be what others are, and miss God's plan for who he wants you to be. You might end up thinking that you are better than someone else, and become arrogant. You might want to do what others are doing, and be led into sin. A better plan is just to keep your eyes on Jesus, the perfect standard of comparison.

God's Challenge

Examine yourselves to see if your faith is really genuine. Test yourselves.   *2 Corinthians 13:5*

Body of Christ

Why is it a waste of time to compare ourselves to others?

God's Response

The human body has many parts, but the many parts make up only one body. So it is with the body of Christ. . . . If the foot says, "I am not a part of the body because I am not a hand," that does not make it any less a part of the body. . . . But God made our bodies with many parts, and he has put each part just where he wants it. *1 Corinthians 12:12, 15, 18*

THE CHURCH IS CALLED THE "body of Christ" or the "body of believers," and is often likened to a person's physical body in which every part has its specific function. It is foolish to try to determine whether your hand or your foot is more important—you need both. God created you and every other believer to serve a certain role in his Kingdom. Only when you work together will God's Kingdom grow and flourish!

God's Promise

Be sure to do what you should, for then you will enjoy the personal satisfaction of having done your work well, and you won't need to compare yourself to anyone else. *Galatians 6:4*

Comparisons

How can I avoid comparing myself to others?

God's Response

Peter turned around and saw the disciple Jesus loved following. . . . Peter asked Jesus, "What about him, Lord?"

Jesus replied, "If I want him to remain alive until I return, what is that to you? You follow me." *John 21:20-22*

YOUR LIFE CAN'T BE COMPARED to someone else's because God created you as a unique individual. When you find your special, God-given purpose, you will not want to be like someone else. When Peter asked Jesus about his fellow disciple John, Jesus told him not to be concerned about anyone else, but just to follow him. Keeping his eyes on Jesus would take Peter exactly where Jesus wanted him to go. In the same way, Jesus calls you to travel your own distinctive road with him.

God's Promise

To enjoy your work and accept your lot in life—that is indeed a gift from God. People who do this rarely look with sorrow on the past, for God has given them reasons for joy. *Ecclesiastes 5:19-20*

Maturity

How can I reach the spiritual maturity I desire?

God's Response

I couldn't talk to you as I would to mature Christians. . . .
I had to feed you with milk and not with solid food.
1 Corinthians 3:1-2

It's like this: When I was a child, I spoke and thought and
reasoned as a child does. But when I grew up, I put away
childish things.   *1 Corinthians 13:11*

S PIRITUAL GROWTH IS like physical growth—you start
small and grow one day at a time. As you grow, however, you need more nourishment. Spiritually you get
this by challenging your mind to study God's Word, ask
questions about it, and seek answers through prayer, the
counsel of other believers, and life's experiences. Look at
each day as a building block, and before you know it, you
will be on your way to spiritual maturity.

God's Challenge

Let us stop going over the basics of Christianity again
and again. Let us go on instead and become mature in
our understanding.   *Hebrews 6:1*

Self-Discipline

How does self-discipline help me to grow?

God's Response

King Solomon became richer and wiser than any other king in all the earth. . . . Now King Solomon loved many foreign women. . . . The LORD had clearly instructed his people not to intermarry with those nations, because the women they married would lead them to worship their gods. . . . In Solomon's old age, [these women] turned his heart to worship their gods instead of trusting only in the LORD his God. . . . Thus, Solomon did what was evil in the LORD's sight.   *1 Kings 10:23; 11:1-2, 4, 6*

WE ARE GIVEN THE GIFT of salvation so that we can grow to resemble Christ and serve others with his love. God wants to produce his character of active love in us, but this requires effort and self-discipline from us. When we make a conscious effort every day to yield our decisions and behavior to the control of God's Holy Spirit, we can resist temptation and grow spiritually. If we don't pay attention, we can easily give control over to the Tempter and fall victim to his schemes.

God's Promise

God has not given us a spirit of fear and timidity, but of power, love, and self-discipline.   *2 Timothy 1:7*

Self-Discipline

How can I cultivate the discipline to obey God?

God's Response

Commit yourselves wholeheartedly to these words of mine. Tie them to your hands and wear them on your forehead as reminders. Teach them to your children. Talk about them when you are at home and when you are on the road, when you are going to bed and when you are getting up. Write them on the doorposts of your house. *Deuteronomy 11:18-20 (NLT2)*

FOR MOST OF US, IT IS DIFFICULT to make obedience a daily habit; we are often tempted to give in to those sins that we most enjoy. Here are four principles in the discipline of obedience: (1) Focus on Scripture, reading and reciting it daily. (2) Teach Scripture to others, adults or children. This helps us to apply it to our lives. (3) Talk about the Bible and spiritual topics every chance you get. Tell others what God means to you. (4) Keep a spiritual diary or journal, writing down Scripture passages and what you learn from them. If you follow these four principles every day, you will come to love obedience and it will become a part of your everyday life.

God's Challenge

Be earnest and disciplined in your prayers.   *1 Peter 4:7*

Setbacks

How do I keep going in the face of setbacks?

God's Response

When the traders came by, his brothers pulled Joseph out of the pit and sold him for twenty pieces of silver, and the Ishmaelite traders took him along to Egypt.   *Genesis 37:28*

After hearing his wife's story, Potiphar was furious! He took Joseph and threw him into the prison where the king's prisoners were held.   *Genesis 39:19-20*

Pharaoh's cup-bearer, however, promptly forgot all about Joseph, never giving him another thought.   *Genesis 40:23*

JOSEPH EXPERIENCED A SERIES of heartbreaking setbacks—being sold into slavery by his brothers, being framed as a rapist by Potiphar's wife, and being forgotten by the cupbearer whose dream Joseph had properly interpreted. While these bad experiences were not sent by God, Joseph understood that God would use them to prepare him for an important assignment later on. Looking at setbacks from that perspective keeps you alert to what you can learn from them and helps you endure them.

God's Promise

As far as I am concerned, God turned into good what you meant for evil.   *Genesis 50:20*

Problems

How does God view my problems?

God's Response

Late that night, the disciples were in their boat in the middle of the lake, and Jesus . . . saw that they were in serious trouble . . . struggling against the wind and waves. . . . Jesus came toward them, walking on the water. . . . Then he climbed into the boat, and the wind stopped.   *Mark 6:47-48, 51 (NLT2)*

WHEN WE READ THIS STORY, we tend to focus only on the miracle of Jesus walking on water. The miracle is so dramatic that our attention is drawn away from the twelve men floundering in a stormy sea. Their boat is sinking. They are exhausted and frightened. Have you ever felt like that? Jesus came to bring them a message. "Don't be afraid," he said. The real miracle is the extraordinary lengths to which Jesus will go in order to comfort us in troubled seas. He understands your trouble and will come to you.

God's Promise

We know that God causes everything to work together for the good of those who love God and are called according to his purpose for them.   *Romans 8:28*

Impatience

What common mistake might I make in handling my problems?

God's Response

Sarai, Abram's wife, had no children. So Sarai took her servant, an Egyptian woman named Hagar, and gave her to Abram so she could bear his children.   *Genesis 16:1-2*

ONE COMMON MISTAKE is giving in to impatience. You may trust that God will handle the situation, but when the answer seems slow in coming, you may decide that God needs a bit of help. Sarai knew that she was to have a child, but God waited twenty-five years to make this promise come true. In the meantime, Sarai took matters into her own hands and created a mess. When you trust God, you must trust him completely, even if it means having to wait.

God's Promise

These things I plan won't happen right away. Slowly, steadily, surely, the time approaches when the vision will be fulfilled. If it seems slow, wait patiently, for it will surely take place. It will not be delayed.
Habakkuk 2:3

Negativity

How can I keep my problems from giving me a bad attitude?

God's Response

After exploring the land for forty days, the men . . . reported to the whole community what they had seen and showed them the fruit they had taken from the land. This was their report to Moses: "We arrived in the land you sent us to see, and it is indeed a magnificent country. . . . But the people living there are powerful, and their cities and towns are fortified and very large. We also saw the descendants of Anak who are living there!" *Numbers 13:25-28*

WHEN YOU'RE FOCUSED on your problem, you can't see the bigger picture of what God might be doing. The Israelites certainly had reason to be afraid, but they forgot that God had already promised to give them the land. Their fear made them negative. As hard as it is, keep your problems in God's perspective so you won't become negative and give up.

God's Promise

Caleb tried to encourage the people as they stood before Moses. "Let's go at once to take the land," he said. "We can certainly conquer it!" *Numbers 13:30*

Problems

How can I learn and grow from my problems?

God's Response

We try to live in such a way that no one will be hindered from finding the Lord by the way we act. . . . We patiently endure troubles and hardships and calamities of every kind. . . . We have proved ourselves by our purity, our understanding, our patience, our kindness, our sincere love, and the power of the Holy Spirit. We have faithfully preached the truth. God's power has been working in us. . . . We serve God whether people honor us or despise us, whether they slander us or praise us. . . . Our hearts ache, but we always have joy. We are poor, but we give spiritual riches to others. We own nothing, and yet we have everything.   *2 Corinthians 6:3-8, 10*

WE GROW THE MOST WHEN we have problems, because that is when our character is stretched. We have to develop patience, purity, kindness, and a host of other Christlike character traits while dealing with a problem. That's a tall order, but if we endure, we will come out stronger and better prepared when the next problem rolls along.

God's Promise

God blesses the people who patiently endure testing. Afterward they will receive the crown of life that God has promised to those who love him.   *James 1:12*

Helping Others

How can I help others in the midst of their problems?

God's Response

This is the message we have heard from the beginning: We should love one another.   *1 John 3:11*

You have done well to share with me in my present difficulty.   *Philippians 4:14*

All praise to the God and Father of our Lord Jesus Christ. He is the source of every mercy and the God who comforts us. He comforts us in all our troubles so that we can comfort others. When others are troubled, we will be able to give them the same comfort God has given us. *2 Corinthians 1:3-4*

WHEN OTHERS ARE FACING PROBLEMS, you can genuinely love them with your actions, emotions, attitudes, words, and presence. The comfort you have received from God in your times of trouble can be passed on to others in need.

God's Challenge

Share each other's troubles and problems, and in this way obey the law of Christ.   *Galatians 6:2*

Overcoming

How can I overcome the problems I face in life?

God's Response

I am the LORD, the God of all the peoples of the world. Is anything too hard for me? *Jeremiah 32:27*

This is what the LORD Almighty says: All this may seem impossible to you now, a small and discouraged remnant of God's people. But do you think this is impossible for me, the LORD Almighty? *Zechariah 8:6*

Jesus looked at them intently and said, "Humanly speaking, it is impossible. But with God everything is possible." *Matthew 19:26*

TOO OFTEN OUR OWN LIMITATIONS cause us to doubt God's ability to work through us. We make excuses for why we think things won't happen instead of thinking about how they might happen, especially when we follow an almighty God! The next time you think a promise from God is impossible, or you are facing a seemingly impossible problem, look at the issue again from God's perspective. Ask him to do the impossible in you.

God's Promise

Nothing is impossible with God. *Luke 1:37*

Extraordinary

I'm just an ordinary person; there's nothing special about me. Why would God use me?

God's Response

The members of the council were amazed when they saw the boldness of Peter and John, for they could see that they were ordinary men who had had no special training. They also recognized them as men who had been with Jesus.   *Acts 4:13*

Live in harmony with each other. Don't try to act important, but enjoy the company of ordinary people.   *Romans 12:16*

WHILE GOD SOMETIMES USES MIRACLES and angels, he more often chooses ordinary people doing ordinary things to accomplish something extraordinary. One day God may call you to do something extraordinary, but meanwhile, get to work serving and obeying him. Then you'll be ready when he calls.

God's Promise

God deliberately chose things the world considers foolish in order to shame those who think they are wise. And he chose those who are powerless to shame those who are powerful.   *1 Corinthians 1:27*

Balance

The months ahead look very busy.
How can I keep a good balance?

God's Response

There is a time for everything, a season for every activity
under heaven.   *Ecclesiastes 3:1*

I brought glory to you here on earth by doing everything
you told me to do. And now, Father, bring me into the
glory we shared before the world began.   *John 17:4-5*

JESUS DID NOT HEAL EVERY sick person in the land, or
convince every person to follow him, or meet every
person he could have if he had lived longer. And yet he
said he did everything God told him to do! God does not
ask you to do everything, just everything he has called you
to do, and he assures you that there is time for whatever
this is. A balanced life honors God, others, and yourself by
the way that you use your gifts, time, and other resources.

God's Promise

If you are wise and understand God's ways, live a life of
steady goodness so that only good deeds will pour forth.
And if you don't brag about the good you do, then you
will be truly wise!   *James 3:13*

Time

How can I make the best use of my time?

God's Response

Teach us to make the most of our time, so that we may grow in wisdom.   *Psalm 90:12*

Be careful how you live, not as fools but as those who are wise. Make the most of every opportunity for doing good in these evil days. Don't act thoughtlessly, but try to understand what the Lord wants you to do. . . . Let the Holy Spirit fill and control you.   *Ephesians 5:15-18*

TIME IS A GIFT. God gives you time so that you have the opportunity to serve him. Valuing time begins with seeing it from God's perspective. When you do so, you learn that there is always time to accomplish God's plans for your life. When you give your time to the Lord, he promises that no opportunity will be wasted.

God's Challenge

How do you know what will happen tomorrow? For your life is like the morning fog—it's here a little while, then it's gone.   *James 4:14*

Time

How can I find the time I need?

God's Response

Remember to observe the Sabbath day by keeping it holy. Six days a week are set apart for your daily duties and regular work, but the seventh day is a day of rest dedicated to the LORD your God. . . . For in six days the LORD made the heavens, the earth, the sea, and everything in them; then he rested on the seventh day. That is why the LORD blessed the Sabbath day and set it apart as holy.   *Exodus 20:8-11*

B ELIEVE IT OR NOT, the best way to have the time you need is to devote time to God for worship and to yourself for rest. Devoting time to God gives you spiritual refreshment and the opportunity to hear his priorities for you. Devoting time to rest gives you physical refreshment and the energy to do what you are called to do.

God's Promise

He said to them, "The Sabbath was made to benefit people, and not people to benefit the Sabbath."
Mark 2:27

Planning

I want to plan my time well, so what is the best way to do that?

God's Response

"Every part of this plan," David told Solomon, "was given to me in writing from the hand of the LORD." *1 Chronicles 28:19*

Three days after my arrival at Jerusalem, I slipped out during the night, taking only a few others with me. I had not told anyone about the plans God had put in my heart for Jerusalem. *Nehemiah 2:11-12*

FIRST, **FOLLOW THE GUIDELINES** for right living that God has revealed in his Word. Then, when you make your plans, you will not move into something that would displease him. Making plans without referring to God and his will is a recipe for frustration and disaster. The path of obedience will always take you in the right direction. If you leave God out of your plans, he may leave you out of his.

God's Promise

Wise planning will watch over you. Understanding will keep you safe. *Proverbs 2:11*

Planning

Doesn't planning ahead conflict with trusting God to lead me?

God's Response

A prudent person foresees the danger ahead and takes precautions; the simpleton goes blindly on and suffers the consequences.   *Proverbs 22:3*

Look here, you people who say, "Today or tomorrow we are going to a certain town and will stay there a year. We will do business there and make a profit." How do you know what will happen tomorrow? For your life is like the morning fog—it's here a little while, then it's gone. What you ought to say is, "If the Lord wants us to, we will live and do this or that." Otherwise you will be boasting about your own plans, and all such boasting is evil.   *James 4:13-16*

PLANNING HELPS YOU PUT YOUR FAITH into action. It demonstrates your desire to use your time wisely and makes you a good steward of the time and resources God has given you. So make your plans, but hold them loosely so that you can adjust if God gives you new marching orders.

God's Promise

You can make many plans, but the LORD's purpose will prevail.   *Proverbs 19:21*

Right Motives

*As I consider my plans for the upcoming months,
how can I have right motives in the activities
I am considering?*

God's Response

May the words of my mouth and the thoughts of my heart
be pleasing to you, O Lord, my rock and my redeemer.
Psalm 19:14

Put me on trial, Lord, and cross-examine me. Test my
motives and affections.   *Psalm 26:2*

Search me, O God, and know my heart; test me and know
my thoughts.   *Psalm 139:23*

PEOPLE OFTEN GET STRESSED OUT because they have
taken on activities and responsibilities for the wrong
reasons. As you consider upcoming involvements, ask
God to help you do things with the right motives and to
reveal any area where they are less than pure. With that
understanding, you will know better which activities you
should be involved in, and which ones you should say
no to.

God's Promise

People may think they are doing what is right, but the
Lord examines the heart.   *Proverbs 21:2*

Wrong Motives

How can I identify wrong motives as I plan ahead?

God's Response

Jealousy and selfishness are not God's kind of wisdom. Such things are earthly, unspiritual, and motivated by the Devil. *James 3:15*

WRONG MOTIVES FOR TAKING ON certain activities might include the desire for money or ambition at the expense of a relationship, doing something simply to show off, the need to look sincere (when you're not), or the need to be admired by people. Take time to pray and honestly consider the motives behind your activities, including the activities you've chosen for your family. If your motives are to please God and serve others, then your actions will please him as well.

God's Promise

Be careful not to jump to conclusions before the Lord returns as to whether or not someone is faithful. When the Lord comes, he will bring our deepest secrets to light and will reveal our private motives. And then God will give to everyone whatever praise is due.
1 Corinthians 4:5

Right Motives

What are some right motives?

God's Response

When they came to the other side, Elijah said to Elisha, "What can I do for you before I am taken away?"

And Elisha replied, "Please let me become your rightful successor." *2 Kings 2:9*

GOD IS PLEASED WHEN YOU SERVE HIM simply because you want to. Wanting to follow in the footsteps of a godly person as Elisha did is a noble motive, as is desiring to serve God and to do your work well. God wants you to act out of love for him. One of the ways to test your motives is to ask yourself why you are considering an activity. If the answer that pops into your head is that you want to help or serve others in some way, that is a good reason to get involved. If your answer involves status, reward, or recognition, you have the wrong motives.

God's Promise

We speak as messengers who have been approved by God to be entrusted with the Good News. Our purpose is to please God, not people. He is the one who examines the motives of our hearts. *1 Thessalonians 2:4*

Meaning

With all that I need to do every day, how can I make sure that my life has meaning?

God's Response

My life is worth nothing unless I use it for doing the work assigned me by the Lord Jesus—the work of telling others the Good News about God's wonderful kindness and love.   *Acts 20:24*

I take joy in doing your will, my God, for your law is written on my heart.   *Psalm 40:8*

YOU DON'T NEED TO DO EARTHSHAKING things in order to have a meaningful life. Your life has meaning when you do the work that God has given you to do. Whether you are changing diapers, running a company, or evangelizing the world, when you do it as though God is doing it through you, your life has meaning because you are sharing the love of God with everyone you see in your circle of influence.

God's Challenge

Here is my final conclusion: Fear God and obey his commands, for this is the duty of every person. *Ecclesiastes 12:13*

Purpose

How can I more fully understand the meaning of my life?

God's Response

Cry out for insight and understanding. Search for them as you would for lost money or hidden treasure. *Proverbs 2:3-4*

I cry out to God Most High, to God who will fulfill his purpose for me. *Psalm 57:2*

UNDERSTANDING THE DEEP TRUTH of life doesn't just happen; you have to search for it. You have to want to know why God made you and put you where you are. If your best friend gave you a letter before leaving on a trip and said, "Read this before I get back," you would read it right away. God has left you not just a letter but a book and has said, "Read this before I return, because it tells you exactly what you need to know to have a purposeful life." Will you read it?

God's Promise

All Scripture is inspired by God and is useful to teach us what is true. . . . It is God's way of preparing us in every way, fully equipped for every good thing God wants us to do. *2 Timothy 3:16-17*

God's Approval

What brings God's approval?

God's Response

The LORD approves of those who are good, but he condemns those who plan wickedness.   *Proverbs 12:2*

It is not merely knowing the law that brings God's approval. Those who obey the law will be declared right in God's sight.   *Romans 2:13*

There is only one God, and there is only one way of being accepted by him. He makes people right with himself only by faith, whether they are Jews or Gentiles.   *Romans 3:30*

BELIEVING THAT GOD IS who he says he is and obeying his Word bring God's approval. With all of your busyness and activities, don't forget what is most important—God and your relationship with him.

God's Promise

There is really only one thing worth being concerned about. Mary has discovered it—and I won't take it away from her.   *Luke 10:42*

God's Approval

Do I have to earn God's approval?

God's Response

When I tried to keep the law, I realized I could never earn God's approval.   *Galatians 2:19*

There is going to come a time of testing at the judgment day to see what kind of work each builder has done. Everyone's work will be put through the fire to see whether or not it keeps its value. If the work survives the fire, that builder will receive a reward. But if the work is burned up, the builder will suffer great loss. The builders themselves will be saved, but like someone escaping through a wall of flames.   *1 Corinthians 3:13-15*

I**T'S NOT WHAT YOU DO FOR GOD**, but your relationship with him that is most important. God's approval of you is based on your personal faith in Jesus Christ, not on your performance. How you live your life matters, of course, but that is not what saves you. Instead, your actions are a by-product of your love for God, and your life reveals your gratitude for what God has done.

God's Promise

Accept each other just as Christ has accepted you; then God will be glorified.   *Romans 15:7*

Busyness

Even if I am careful to check my motives and plan carefully, my life is still very busy. Is that good or bad?

God's Response

She is energetic and strong, a hard worker. . . . She carefully watches all that goes on in her household and does not have to bear the consequences of laziness.   *Proverbs 31:17, 27*

Be sure to stay busy and plant a variety of crops, for you never know which will grow—perhaps they all will. *Ecclesiastes 11:6*

RICH HARVESTS CANNOT COME from lazy fingers. Getting the job done will require work. Activities only become dangerous if busyness replaces real accomplishment or if you are neglecting God or the people in your care. It is a good thing to be successful through honesty, hard work, and good treatment of others. It is even better to use your resources to help those in need, to support God's church, and to make a spiritual impact on society. We should all be busy doing that.

God's Promise

Lazy people want much but get little, but those who work hard will prosper and be satisfied.   *Proverbs 13:4*

Success

Does God want me to be successful in the work I do?

God's Response

A Jew named Aquila . . . had recently arrived from Italy with his wife, Priscilla. . . . Paul lived and worked with them, for they were tentmakers just as he was.   *Acts 18:2-3*

Work hard. . . . As slaves of Christ, do the will of God with all your heart. Work with enthusiasm, as though you were working for the Lord rather than for people. *Ephesians 6:6-7*

G OD ENDORSES HARD WORK, ingenuity, and success. Paul, Aquila, and Priscilla were Christian leaders in ministry and in business. The quality of your work and your enthusiasm for it reveal the nature of your commitment to Christ. Hard work done with excellence and integrity honors God and may bring material resources that can be used for God's glory. God also recognizes that hard work does not always lead to material success. What is important is that we do our work as though God were our boss.

God's Promise

Commit your work to the LORD, and then your plans will succeed.   *Proverbs 16:3*

Work

What principles should guide my work?

God's Response

Whatever you do, do well.   *Ecclesiastes 9:10*

Do not cheat or rob anyone. Always pay your hired workers promptly.   *Leviticus 19:13*

The LORD demands fairness in every business deal; he sets the standard.   *Proverbs 16:11*

AT ITS BEST, WORK HONORS GOD and brings meaning and joy to life. We should emulate the character traits we see in God's work, such as excellence, concern for the well-being of others, purpose, beauty, and service. When you have the perspective that you are actually working for God, it takes the focus away from the task and onto why you are doing it—to help people know God. The excitement and interest that come from working for God are not primarily from the work but from the One for whom we do the work.

God's Challenge

Yes, use honest weights and measures, so that you will enjoy a long life in the land the LORD your God is giving you. Those who cheat with dishonest weights and measures are detestable to the LORD your God.
Deuteronomy 25:15-16

Work

What if my work has nothing to do with anything "Christian"—how can God be glorified in my work?

God's Response

Having finished his task, God rested from all his work. . . . The LORD God placed the man in the Garden of Eden to tend and care for it.   *Genesis 2:2, 15*

WORK IS ANCHORED in God's very character. Part of being made in God's image is sharing in the industrious and creative aspects of his nature. Gardening was the very first job a human had. Christians are needed in all kinds of vocations. Whatever your job, believe that God has placed you there for a reason, and then do your work well as a service to God and as a way to allow others to see his love in action through you.

God's Promise

This should be your ambition: to live a quiet life, minding your own business and working with your hands, just as we commanded you before. As a result, people who are not Christians will respect the way you live, and you will not need to depend on others to meet your financial needs.   *1 Thessalonians 4:11-12*

Routine

*As I settle into the activities of this season,
what should always be a part of my routine?*

God's Response

You must commit yourselves wholeheartedly to these
commands I am giving you today. Repeat them again
and again to your children. Talk about them when you
are at home and when you are away on a journey, when
you are lying down and when you are getting up again.
Deuteronomy 6:6-7

Daniel . . . prayed three times a day, just as he had always
done, giving thanks to his God.   *Daniel 6:10*

As was Paul's custom, he went to the synagogue service.
Acts 17:2

YOUR ROUTINE SHOULD ALWAYS include reading God's
Word and sharing it with friends or family, praying,
and attending church. Make these activities a priority, for
you need them in order to have the peace, patience, and
strength for everything else you do!

God's Promise

I will bless you every day, and I will praise you forever.
Psalm 145:2

Church

Do I really need to go to church?

God's Response

The church is his body; it is filled by Christ, who fills everything everywhere with his presence.   *Ephesians 1:23*

The human body has many parts, but the many parts make up only one body. So it is with the body of Christ. Some of us are Jews, some are Gentiles.   *1 Corinthians 12:12-13*

Let us not neglect our meeting together, as some people do, but encourage and warn each other.   *Hebrews 10:25*

ALL BELIEVERS TOGETHER form God's family, and only by meeting together can we bond. The church exists in part to equip God's people to do God's work by encouraging them in their faith. At church, Christians learn to work together in unity and to practice reconciliation between different people in a way that is only possible by Christ's Spirit. When we meet together, we can build each other up and help each other. The church needs you, for the body of Christ is not complete unless you are there!

God's Promise

Upon this rock I will build my church, and all the powers of hell will not conquer it.   *Matthew 16:18*

Church

Why is it important for me to be involved in the church?

God's Response

Just as our bodies have many parts and each part has a special function, so it is with Christ's body. We are all parts of his one body, and each of us has different work to do. And since we are all one body in Christ . . . each of us needs all the others. God has given each of us the ability to do certain things well. *Romans 12:4-6*

GOD HAS GIVEN GIFTS TO EACH OF US. Some of us are great organizers and administrators, while others are gifted musicians, teachers, and dishwashers. When everyone in the congregation uses their gifts to serve, the church becomes a powerful force for good, a strong witness for Jesus, and a mighty army to combat Satan's attacks against God's people in your community.

God's Promise

What good fellowship we enjoyed as we walked together to the house of God. *Psalm 55:14*

Fellowship

Why do I need the fellowship of other believers?

God's Response

When he arrived and saw this proof of God's favor, he was filled with joy, and he encouraged the believers to stay true to the Lord.   *Acts 11:23*

Use his words to teach and counsel each other. Sing psalms and hymns and spiritual songs to God with thankful hearts.   *Colossians 3:16*

Since we are all one body in Christ, we belong to each other, and each of us needs all the others.   *Romans 12:5*

GOD CREATED YOU FOR RELATIONSHIP. You cannot grow as a believer all by yourself, without other Christians around you. Fellowship with other believers is necessary to keep you accountable, to help you learn God's Word correctly, to pray for each other's needs, to encourage one another, and to help you mature in your faith.

God's Promise

If we are living in the light of God's presence, just as Christ is, then we have fellowship with each other, and the blood of Jesus, his Son, cleanses us from every sin.
1 John 1:7

Finding Depth

How is Christian fellowship different from other kinds of friendship?

God's Response

I'm eager to encourage you in your faith, but I also want to be encouraged by yours. In this way, each of us will be a blessing to the other.   *Romans 1:12*

Confess your sins to each other and pray for each other so that you may be healed.   *James 5:16*

GOOD FRIENDS ARE A WONDERFUL GIFT. Fellowship among believers in Jesus (at church or in small groups) is unique because it invites the living God into your midst. People gather with a common perspective on life because they know their sins have been forgiven and that this affects their freedom and their future. Christian fellowship provides a place for honest sharing about the things in life that really matter, encouragement to stay strong in the face of temptation and persecution, and supernatural help in dealing with problems.

God's Promise

Where two or three gather together because they are mine, I am there among them.   *Matthew 18:20*

Annoyance

What if I just don't like some other Christians?
Some can be pretty annoying.

God's Response

Don't just pretend that you love others. Really love them. . . .
Take delight in honoring each other. . . . Don't try to act
important, but enjoy the company of ordinary people. And
don't think you know it all!   *Romans 12:9-10, 16*

I T'S EASY TO LIKE PEOPLE who are likable, but we model
more of God's love when we serve those who are annoying. You'll never find a perfect church, and you'll never find
a perfect group of people—even among Christians—so
don't go looking for that. Instead, seek God's guidance as
to where you should be, and then take joy in reaching out
and loving those God has placed in your sphere of influence. You may be surprised at how the power of God can
bring the most unlikely people together as friends. When
you reach out to others in love, your heart is also changed.

God's Challenge

If we are living now by the Holy Spirit, let us follow the
Holy Spirit's leading in every part of our lives. Let us not
become conceited, or irritate one another, or be jealous
of one another.   *Galatians 5:25-26*

Aggravation

How should I handle it when people aggravate me?

God's Response

Those who control their anger have great understanding; those with a hasty temper will make mistakes. A relaxed attitude lengthens life; jealousy rots it away. *Proverbs 14:29-30*

My dear brothers and sisters, be quick to listen, slow to speak, and slow to get angry. *James 1:19*

AGGRAVATION IS REALLY a slow-burning anger. The more aggravated you get, the more angry you become until finally you lash out. Suddenly you can be more guilty before God than the one who aggravated you! It is important to recognize aggravation before it gets out of control. When you are aggravated at someone, try these helpful steps—pray for that person, think of something good in that person, and get to know that person. When you learn why they behave a certain way, you may find your aggravation turning to compassion.

God's Challenge

Love is not irritable, and it keeps no record of when it has been wronged. *1 Corinthians 13:5*

Hurt

How should I deal with people who have hurt me?

God's Response

Since God chose you to be the holy people whom he loves, you must clothe yourselves with tenderhearted mercy, kindness, humility, gentleness, and patience. You must make allowance for each other's faults and forgive the person who offends you. Remember, the Lord forgave you, so you must forgive others. *Colossians 3:12-13*

WHEN GOD FORGIVES YOU, he wipes away the past and remembers it no more, so you should not remember it either. Forgiveness deletes the sin file from the hard drive. The only thing that is within your control in dealing with people who have hurt you is to ask God to help you to forgive. Forgiveness releases the bitterness from your soul and begins to heal the hurt. You must remember that your sin has deeply hurt God, yet he forgives you and is ready to restore his relationship with you. You must follow his example, or you will live with a bitter spirit.

God's Promise

When you are praying, first forgive anyone you are holding a grudge against, so that your Father in heaven will forgive your sins, too. *Mark 11:25*

Apology

How do I make things right when I have hurt someone?

God's Response

It's harder to make amends with an offended friend than to capture a fortified city. Arguments separate friends like a gate locked with iron bars.   *Proverbs 18:19*

I will go home to my father and say, "Father, I have sinned against both heaven and you."   *Luke 15:18*

ALTHOUGH MAKING AMENDS for an offense may be difficult, your relationships with others are worth your immediate and diligent efforts. "I'm sorry" are two very important words. When you have hurt someone, apologize as quickly as possible and make any needed restitution. Forgiveness is powerful because it frees both sides from bitterness.

God's Challenge

If you are standing before the altar in the Temple, offering a sacrifice to God, and you suddenly remember that someone has something against you, leave your sacrifice there beside the altar. Go and be reconciled to that person. Then come and offer your sacrifice to God. *Matthew 5:23-24*

Bitterness

What should I do with the bitterness I feel?

God's Response

When you are praying, first forgive anyone you are holding a grudge against, so that your Father in heaven will forgive your sins, too.   *Mark 11:25*

AFTER SOMEONE HAS WRONGED YOU, time will either harden your heart, making you bitter and unyielding, or it will soften it, giving you a desire to restore the relationship. If someone has betrayed you recently, is your heart growing hard, or are you willing to yield for the sake of peace? When Jesus was asked how many times we should forgive others, he said, "seventy times seven" (Matthew 18:22). Perhaps he meant that constant willingness to forgive is the only way to mend a bitter spirit and achieve healing and restoration.

God's Challenge

Get rid of all bitterness, rage, anger, harsh words, and slander, as well as all types of malicious behavior. Instead, be kind to each other, tenderhearted, forgiving one another, just as God through Christ has forgiven you.
Ephesians 4:31-32

Tragedy

Where is God in the pain of my tragedy?

God's Response

Elimelech died and Naomi was left with her two sons. . . . About ten years later, both Mahlon and Kilion died. This left Naomi alone, without her husband or sons. . . . "Call me Mara," [she said] . . . "Why should you call me Naomi when the LORD has caused me to suffer and the Almighty has sent such tragedy?"   *Ruth 1:3-5, 20-21*

When your faith is tested, your endurance has a chance to grow. . . . When your endurance is fully developed, you will be strong in character and ready for anything.   *James 1:3-4*

THE UNIVERSAL HUMAN RESPONSE to calamity is panic, fear, and grief. The Bible teaches that Christians, people who live in relationship with God through Jesus Christ, also grieve during times of loss—but that we grieve with hope. We grieve because we experience the real pain of loss, but we grieve with hope because we know that God can and will redeem our tragedy into his glory. God does not waste our sorrows.

God's Promise

In my distress I prayed to the LORD, and the LORD answered me and rescued me.   *Psalm 118:5*

Tragedy

How should I handle tragedy?

God's Response

People can never predict when hard times might come. Like fish in a net or birds in a snare, people are often caught by sudden tragedy.   *Ecclesiastes 9:12*

LORD, be merciful to us, for we have waited for you. Be our strength each day and our salvation in times of trouble. *Isaiah 33:2*

SOMETIMES THE SUFFERING THAT COMES to us through tragedy is not our fault. It just happens. How we react to suffering is critical. We live in a fallen world where sin is often allowed to run its course, affecting both believers and nonbelievers (Matthew 5:45). God doesn't want to see us suffer, but the great message of the Bible is that he promises to bring renewal, healing, and spiritual maturity through it so that we can be stronger and better equipped to help others and to live with purpose and meaning.

God's Promise

You need not be afraid of disaster or the destruction that comes upon the wicked, for the LORD is your security. He will keep your foot from being caught in a trap. *Proverbs 3:25-26*

Crisis

What are some of the blessings that can come from my times of crisis?

God's Response

I want you to know, dear brothers and sisters, that everything that has happened to me here has helped to spread the Good News.   *Philippians 1:12*

The people who walk in darkness will see a great light—a light that will shine on all who live in the land where death casts its shadow.   *Isaiah 9:2*

GOD'S TRANSFORMING POWER often touches you most deeply in times of crisis. Sometimes a crisis helps to clear away the mundane clutter so that you see your life and its priorities more clearly. How you react to times of crisis shows your character and can determine what others think about Christ. While it might be hard to believe now, you can trust that God will bring light back into your darkness. Without God, you have no hope, and no value can come of your suffering.

God's Promise

These trials will make you partners with Christ in his suffering.   *1 Peter 4:13*

Pain

How does God help me deal with my pain?

God's Response

In all their suffering he also suffered, and he personally rescued them. In his love and mercy he redeemed them. He lifted them up and carried them through all the years.
Isaiah 63:9

The Holy Spirit helps us in our distress. For we don't even know what we should pray for, nor how we should pray. But the Holy Spirit prays for us with groanings that cannot be expressed in words. *Romans 8:26*

IT IS EASER TO DEAL WITH PAIN when someone is helping you through it. God feels your pain. He knows what you are going through and is in the best position to help you. He wants you to put your pain on his shoulders so he can bear it for you.

God's Promise

Give your burdens to the LORD, and he will take care of you. He will not permit the godly to slip and fall.
Psalm 55:22

Healing

What will heal my pain?

God's Response

Even we Christians, although we have the Holy Spirit within us as a foretaste of future glory, also groan to be released from pain and suffering. We, too, wait anxiously for that day when God will give us our full rights as his children.   *Romans 8:23*

TRUSTING GOD DOES NOT PRODUCE a storybook life here on earth in which every problem is quickly resolved. Sometimes we get sick and don't get better, relationships break down and don't get reconciled, and jobs are lost and not regained. We can rejoice, however, that we are assured of one happy ending, the most important one. When Jesus returns, doubt, disappointment, disease, and death will disappear, and we will live in God's joy forever (Revelation 21:1-4, 22:1-6). Because this happy ending is utterly certain, we can endure the unanswered questions and unending crises of this life.

God's Promise

You have turned my mourning into joyful dancing. You have taken away my clothes of mourning and clothed me with joy, that I might sing praises to you and not be silent.   *Psalm 30:11-12*

Pain

What can I learn from my pain?

God's Response

The sacrifice you want is a broken spirit. A broken and repentant heart, O God, you will not despise.　*Psalm 51:17*

He told them plainly, "Lazarus is dead. And for your sake, I am glad I wasn't there, because this will give you another opportunity to believe in me. Come, let's go see him." *John 11:14-15*

WE CAN LEARN MUCH THROUGH PAIN: (1) Pain can be redemptive—your broken heart can lead you to God through the realization, confession, and repentance of sin. (2) Pain can reveal God's power as you see him respond to your cry for help. (3) Pain can test and prove your commitment to God. Will you move toward him or away from him when you are hurting? (4) Pain equips you to comfort others in their pain because you know what they are going through. Use your pain to strengthen your faith, your character, and your compassion for others.

God's Promise

At least I can take comfort in this: Despite the pain, I have not denied the words of the Holy One.　*Job 6:10*

Character

People say that a Christian should have "good character." What does that mean?

God's Response

You are a holy people, who belong to the LORD your God. Of all the people on earth, [he] has chosen you to be his own special treasure.   *Deuteronomy 7:6*

God created human beings in his own image.
Genesis 1:27 (NLT2)

GOD MADE US IN HIS OWN IMAGE. This makes us unique among God's creatures because we reflect him, including his character traits. We have the potential to be loving, truthful, patient, forgiving, kind, and faithful. Being made in God's image does not mean being a god, or even godly, but it means that we have many of God's characteristics. God must want us to use them as he does, to honor and benefit others.

God's Promise

Those who are wise will shine as bright as the sky, and those who turn many to righteousness will shine like stars forever.   *Daniel 12:3*

Character

Why does character matter?

God's Response

Never let loyalty and kindness get away from you! Wear them like a necklace; write them deep within your heart. Then you will find favor with both God and people, and you will gain a good reputation.   *Proverbs 3:3-4*

When the Holy Spirit controls our lives, he will produce this kind of fruit in us: love, joy, peace, patience, kindness, goodness, faithfulness, gentleness, and self-control. *Galatians 5:22-23*

PEOPLE OFTEN ARGUE THAT someone's personal life does not matter as long as they perform well on the job or look good in public. God, however, does not make a distinction between your public and private life. Justice, righteousness, integrity, mercy, honesty, fairness, and faithfulness are essential traits of a godly person's character because they reflect God's character. You are a person of good character when you display the same godly integrity in private as you do in public.

God's Promise

Even children are known by the way they act, whether their conduct is pure and right.   *Proverbs 20:11*

Character

How is character developed?

God's Response

Remember how the LORD your God led you through the wilderness for forty years, humbling you and testing you to prove your character, and to find out whether or not you would really obey his commands.   *Deuteronomy 8:2*

Obedience is far better than sacrifice. Listening to him is much better than offering the fat of rams.   *1 Samuel 15:22*

YOU WERE NOT BORN WITH a godly character; it is the fruit of a process that evolves only through time, experience, humility, and testing. When you realize that you are not all that you would like to be, when you make a commitment to know God and read his Word, and when you face tough challenges and choices wisely, your character will become a better and better reflection of God's character.

God's Promise

Endurance develops strength of character in us, and character strengthens our confident expectation of salvation.   *Romans 5:4*

Good Fruit

What does the Bible mean when it says that my life should produce "fruit"?

God's Response

When the Holy Spirit controls our lives, he will produce this kind of fruit in us: love, joy, peace, patience, kindness, goodness, faithfulness, gentleness, and self-control. *Galatians 5:22-23*

THE "FRUIT" THE BIBLE talks about is the "fruit of the Spirit," character qualities that the Holy Spirit wants to develop in your life. He will not force you to have these qualities, but when you accept Jesus as Savior, the Holy Spirit comes to live in you. Only he has the power to put your old nature to death, giving you a new nature that produces good fruit, or good character traits. Your life will continue to bear good fruit only when you stay connected to the source of growth.

God's Promise

I am the vine; you are the branches. Those who remain in me, and I in them, will produce much fruit. For apart from me you can do nothing.　*John 15:5*

Love

What is love?

God's Response

Love is patient and kind. Love is not jealous or boastful or proud or rude. Love does not demand its own way. Love is not irritable, and it keeps no record of when it has been wronged. It is never glad about injustice but rejoices whenever the truth wins out. Love never gives up, never loses faith, is always hopeful, and endures through every circumstance.   *1 Corinthians 13:4-7*

A HEALTHY DEFINITION OF LOVE is crucial to understanding the central message of the Bible. According to the Bible, love is not about sexuality, nor is it primarily a feeling. The Bible teaches that love is a commitment, a consistent and determined decision to think of others first, to put their needs above your own, and to serve them first. God loves us in that way and gives us the ability to love others.

God's Promise

There are three things that will endure—faith, hope, and love—and the greatest of these is love.
1 Corinthians 13:13

Childlikeness

How can I do a better job of accepting God's love?

God's Response

"No," Peter protested, "you will never wash my feet!"

Jesus replied, "But if I don't wash you, you won't belong to me."   *John 13:8*

Let the children come to me. Don't stop them! For the Kingdom of God belongs to such as these.   *Luke 18:16*

YOU BEGIN TO ACCEPT GOD'S LOVE as you increase in humility and decrease in self-sufficiency. Jesus encourages you to receive his love with the same kind of trust a little child shows. Receiving God's love is an act of simple faith, but first you have to be humble enough to know that you need God and can't make it through life or eternity without him.

God's Promise

I will be faithful to you and make you mine, and you will finally know me as LORD.   *Hosea 2:20*

Love

How can I be more loving toward others?

God's Response

If anyone says, "I am living in the light," but hates a Christian brother or sister, that person is still living in darkness.   *1 John 2:9*

If we love each other, God lives in us, and his love has been brought to full expression through us.   *1 John 4:12*

We love each other as a result of his loving us first.
1 John 4:19

IF YOU ARE A CHRISTIAN, rejecting another Christian is not an option. You may find a fellow believer to be unlovable, but when you stop to think how unlovable you sometimes make yourself to God without losing his love, you may find it in your heart to be more accepting of others. The only reason we can love others, and they can love us, is because God loved us first—to the point of dying for us. Remembering his great love for you should soften your heart and allow you to love others, even when they don't seem lovable.

God's Promise

Your love for one another will prove to the world that you are my disciples.   *John 13:35*

Loving Your Enemies

What does it mean to love my enemies?

God's Response

You have heard that the law of Moses says, "Love your neighbor" and hate your enemy. But I say, love your enemies! Pray for those who persecute you!   *Matthew 5:43-44*

Don't repay evil for evil. Don't retaliate when people say unkind things about you. Instead, pay them back with a blessing. That is what God wants you to do, and he will bless you for it.   *1 Peter 3:9*

SHOWING LOVE TO ONE'S ENEMIES is always unreasonable—unless you realize that you were once an enemy of God until he forgave you. When you love an enemy, you see him or her as Christ does—as a person in need of grace. Getting to that point requires prayer. You can't pray for someone and not feel compassion for them. This is how you can refrain from retaliating when they hurt you, and this is how God can turn an enemy into a friend.

God's Challenge

If your enemies are hungry, feed them. If they are thirsty, give them something to drink. . . . Don't let evil get the best of you, but conquer evil by doing good.
Romans 12:20-21

What is joy?

God's Response

Let the godly rejoice. Let them be glad in God's presence. Let them be filled with joy.   *Psalm 68:3*

Our hearts ache, but we always have joy. We are poor, but we give spiritual riches to others. We own nothing, and yet we have everything.   *2 Corinthians 6:10*

JOY IS THE CELEBRATION of walking in God's presence. It is an inner happiness that lasts despite the circumstances around you because it is based on a relationship with Jesus Christ. If you are a believer, this gives you absolute confidence that God is real, personal, and involved in your life, that evil will one day be defeated forever, and that heaven is a reality. With this new perspective, you realize that your feelings may go up and down, but joy runs so deep that nothing can take it away.

God's Promise

Those who have been ransomed by the LORD will return to Jerusalem, singing songs of everlasting joy. Sorrow and mourning will disappear, and they will be overcome with joy and gladness.   *Isaiah 51:11*

Joy

Where does joy come from?

God's Response

May all who search for you be filled with joy and gladness. May those who love your salvation repeatedly shout, "The LORD is great!" *Psalm 40:16*

Consider the joy of those corrected by God! Do not despise the chastening of the Almighty when you sin. *Job 5:17*

I know the LORD is always with me. . . . No wonder my heart is filled with joy. *Psalm 16:8-9*

THE LORD HIMSELF IS THE SOURCE of true joy. The more you love him, know him, walk with him, and become like him, the greater your joy will be. Even times of discipline can be considered joyful because you know that God loves you enough to correct you.

God's Promise

The joy of the LORD is your strength! *Nehemiah 8:10*

Joyfulness

How can I be more joyful?

God's Response

Always be full of joy in the Lord. I say it again—rejoice!
Philippians 4:4

I am overcome with joy because of your unfailing love, for you have seen my troubles, and you care about the anguish of my soul.   *Psalm 31:7*

Always be joyful.   *1 Thessalonians 5:16*

THERE ARE AREAS OF THE CHRISTIAN LIFE that are very serious—confronting sin and its consequences, church discipline, fighting evil. But there is also great delight in knowing that the God of the universe loves us, has a plan for us, and has made this wonderful world for us. He tells us to serve him enthusiastically. The Bible urges us to serve God with all of our being, with an enthusiasm that comes from deep within our hearts and souls. Joy and enthusiasm light the fire of service.

God's Promise

You love him even though you have never seen him. Though you do not see him, you trust him; and even now you are happy with a glorious, inexpressible joy.
1 Peter 1:8

He Rejoices

What brings God joy?

God's Response

He led me to a place of safety; he rescued me because he delights in me.   *Psalm 18:19*

The LORD's delight is in those who honor him, those who put their hope in his unfailing love.   *Psalm 147:11*

You are worthy, O Lord our God, to receive glory and honor and power. For you created everything, and it is for your pleasure that they exist and were created. *Revelation 4:11*

YOU BRING GOD JOY when you love him, honor him, and put your hope in him. He rejoices over you with gladness when you commit your life to serving him. Think about it—God's greatest joy is a relationship with you, and that is why he created you. That thought should make you realize your great value.

God's Promise

The LORD your God has arrived to live among you. He is a mighty savior. He will rejoice over you with great gladness. With his love, he will calm all your fears. He will exult over you by singing a happy song. *Zephaniah 3:17*

Backsliding

Why do we forget to stay close to God?

God's Response

Beware that in your plenty you do not forget the LORD your God and disobey his commands. . . . When you have become full and prosperous and have built fine homes to live in . . . be careful. Do not become proud at that time and forget the LORD your God.   *Deuteronomy 8:11-12, 14*

IT'S EASY TO FEEL DISAPPOINTMENT after fulfilling a major commitment. After victory we are most vulnerable. Pride can make us feel overconfident, but when there is no longer a big goal before us, our emotions can take a nosedive. In no time, we can go from elation to discouragement. Here are a few ways to stay close to God: (1) Declare your allegiance to him out loud every day. (2) Choose daily to live the way God wants you to. (3) Obey his Word faithfully and deliberately. (4) Find a place to serve him again right away, and do so with energy and enthusiasm. (5) Learn to rest in the Lord during the down times. If you seek God deliberately each day, it will be hard to forget him.

God's Promise

You will live in joy and peace. The mountains and hills will burst into song, and the trees of the field will clap their hands!   *Isaiah 55:12*

Peace with God

How can I find peace with God?

God's Response

He was wounded and crushed for our sins. He was beaten that we might have peace. He was whipped, and we were healed!   *Isaiah 53:5*

There will be glory and honor and peace from God for all who do good.   *Romans 2:10*

Those who love your law have great peace and do not stumble.   *Psalm 119:165*

TO BE AT PEACE WITH GOD, you have to stop fighting him for control of your life and struggling over his plan for you. After all, he created you—he knows you better than you know yourself, and he knows what is best for you. You will find peace with God when you give up your pride and accept his redemption, not only for your soul, but for your life on earth as well.

God's Promise

Since we have been made right in God's sight by faith, we have peace with God because of what Jesus Christ our Lord has done for us.   *Romans 5:1*

How can I make peace with others?

God's Response

Live in harmony and peace. Then the God of love and peace will be with you.   *2 Corinthians 13:11*

Always keep yourselves united in the Holy Spirit, and bind yourselves together with peace.   *Ephesians 4:3*

Never pay back evil for evil to anyone. . . . Do your part to live in peace with everyone.   *Romans 12:17-18*

TO LIVE PEACEABLY WITH OTHERS does not mean avoiding conflict, but handling conflict appropriately. Conflict handled poorly leads to fractured relationships. Avoiding conflict altogether leads to the same end because there is unresolved hurt or anger. Rather, when conflict arises, rely on the Holy Spirit to keep you calm. Do not retaliate in anger, but respond with love. Do your best to restore harmony.

God's Challenge

Work hard at living in peace with others.   *Psalm 34:14*

World Peace

Is there any hope for world peace?

God's Response

God blesses those who work for peace, for they will be called the children of God.   *Matthew 5:9*

A child is born to us, a son is given to us. . . . These will be his royal titles . . . Prince of Peace.   *Isaiah 9:6*

He will remove all of their sorrows, and there will be no more death or sorrow or crying or pain. For the old world and its evils are gone forever.   *Revelation 21:4*

WAR IS AN INEVITABLE CONSEQUENCE of human sin. Christians are called to pray and work for peace in the world. Just think how much worse it would be if we stopped doing that! However, because of humanity's sinful nature, war will not end until Jesus, the Prince of Peace, returns, and then there will finally be peace forever.

God's Promise

The LORD will settle international disputes. All the nations will beat their swords into plowshares and their spears into pruning hooks. All wars will stop, and military training will come to an end.   *Micah 4:3*

Patience

How can I develop more patience?

God's Response

May God, who gives this patience and encouragement, help you live in complete harmony with each other—each with the attitude of Christ Jesus toward the other.　*Romans 15:5*

Be patient with each other, making allowance for each other's faults because of your love.　*Ephesians 4:2*

PATIENCE AND PERSPECTIVE go hand in hand. When you are always focused on your own agenda and priorities, you will find yourself impatient much of the time because life will rarely go the way you want it to. If you take the larger perspective that life is a journey and not a straight line between two points, you will realize that what you do along the way is as important as getting there. This allows you to patiently wait and learn when things don't go your way, and even to find ways to serve others on the detours of daily life.

God's Promise

Be glad for all God is planning for you. Be patient in trouble, and always be prayerful.　*Romans 12:12*

Impatience

What are some consequences of impatience?

God's Response

Samuel said, "What is this you have done?"

Saul replied, "I saw my men scattering from me, and you didn't arrive when you said you would, and the Philistines are at Micmash ready for battle. So I said, 'The Philistines are ready to march against us, and I haven't even asked for the LORD's help!' So I felt obliged to offer the burnt offering myself before you came."
1 Samuel 13:11-12

GOD USES LIFE CIRCUMSTANCES to develop your patience. Patient waiting is harder than running ahead, but it may keep us from running into disaster. Saul's impatience led him to sin, which caused him to lose his kingdom. Learning to wait is difficult, but the only way to learn patience is to practice it—by waiting!

God's Promise

Don't be impatient for the LORD to act! Travel steadily along his path. He will honor you, giving you the land.
Psalm 37:34

Waiting

What does it mean to "wait on the Lord"?

God's Response

I wait quietly before God, for my salvation comes from him. . . . I wait quietly before God, for my hope is in him. *Psalm 62:1, 5*

I waited patiently for the LORD to help me, and he turned to me and heard my cry.   *Psalm 40:1*

THE ABILITY TO WAIT QUIETLY for something is evidence of a strong character. Waiting on the Lord is the patient confidence that what he promises for our life now and in the future will come true. When we are able to wait quietly for God to act without becoming restless and agitated, we show that we fully trust his timing. What a confident and peaceful way to live!

God's Promise

Those who wait on the LORD will find new strength. They will fly high on wings like eagles. They will run and not grow weary. They will walk and not faint. *Isaiah 40:31*

Kindness

Is kindness overrated? Why should I be kind to others?

God's Response

Love is patient and kind.   *1 Corinthians 13:4*

When you are harvesting your crops and forget to bring in a bundle of grain from your field, don't go back to get it. Leave it for the foreigners, orphans, and widows. Then the LORD your God will bless you in all you do.   *Deuteronomy 24:19*

K INDNESS IS AN ACT OF LOVE, and there is no greater command from God than for us to love one another. It is a simple but profound truth that God blesses you for acts of kindness, and he will bless you in ways that are best for you. You may think that having more money would be a great blessing, but God may know that a close friendship, a deeper relationship with him, or victory over a bad habit would be more valuable. As our kindness toward others blesses them, we in turn will be blessed by God's kindness.

God's Challenge

Never let loyalty and kindness get away from you! Wear them like a necklace; write them deep within your heart.
Proverbs 3:3

Kindness

How can I show kindness to others?

God's Response

Then the way you live will always honor and please the Lord, and you will continually do good, kind things for others. All the while, you will learn to know God better and better.   *Colossians 1:10*

Do for others what you would like them to do for you. *Matthew 7:12*

I myself have gained much joy and comfort from your love, my brother, because your kindness has so often refreshed the hearts of God's people.   *Philemon 1:7*

YOU SHOW KINDNESS BY being pleasant and gracious, always thinking of ways to serve and help others. You can be kind even in a confrontation. Kindness is not a single act but a lifestyle. Practice kindness in all you do and say, always treating others as you would want to be treated. When you do that, you bring great refreshment to everyone you meet and you honor and please the Lord.

God's Promise

Your own soul is nourished when you are kind.
Proverbs 11:17

God's Kindness

How does God show his kindness?

God's Response

God our Savior showed us his kindness and love. He saved us, not because of the good things we did, but because of his mercy. He washed away our sins and gave us a new life through the Holy Spirit. He generously poured out the Spirit upon us because of what Jesus Christ our Savior did. He declared us not guilty because of his great kindness. And now we know that we will inherit eternal life. These things I have told you are all true.   *Titus 3:4-8*

BY GOD'S KINDNESS YOU WERE given the free gift of salvation even though you didn't deserve it. Because of God's kindness, you have forgiveness and freedom from guilt. God's kindness has blessed you beyond your wildest dreams because you have a perfect life secured for all eternity in heaven.

God's Promise

If they are saved by God's kindness, then it is not by their good works. For in that case, God's wonderful kindness would not be what it really is—free and undeserved.   *Romans 11:6*

Goodness

How can I "be good"?

God's Response

She must be well respected by everyone because of the good she has done. . . . Has she been kind to strangers? . . . Has she helped those who are in trouble?   *1 Timothy 5:10*

The Kingdom of God is not a matter of what we eat or drink, but of living a life of goodness and peace and joy in the Holy Spirit.   *Romans 14:17*

GOODNESS IS NOT MERELY being talented at something, as in "she is good at painting." Goodness is a composite of many qualities, such as being kind, helpful, loving, pleasant, generous, and gentle. These qualities exhibit our likeness to God. When Christ takes control of our hearts, we will begin doing good deeds that, when we have practiced them over a lifetime, will be defined as goodness.

God's Promise

You are a chosen people. You are a kingdom of priests, God's holy nation, his very own possession. This is so you can show others the goodness of God, for he called you out of the darkness into his wonderful light.   *1 Peter 2:9*

God's Goodness

In what ways can I see God's goodness?

God's Response

In the beginning God created the heavens and the earth. . . . And God saw that it was good.   *Genesis 1:1, 4*

Surely your goodness and unfailing love will pursue me all the days of my life, and I will live in the house of the LORD forever.   *Psalm 23:6*

The LORD replied, "I will make all my goodness pass before you, and I will call out my name, 'the LORD,' to you. I will show kindness to anyone I choose, and I will show mercy to anyone I choose."   *Exodus 33:19*

GOD'S GOODNESS CAN BE SEEN in creation. He could have created a black-and-white world with no scents, sounds, or tastes, but out of his goodness came incredible beauty and variety. His goodness is also revealed in his kindness and unfailing love for you.

God's Promise

The LORD is wonderfully good to those who wait for him and seek him.   *Lamentations 3:25*

Gratitude

*How can I show my appreciation
for God's goodness to me?*

God's Response

Then I will tell everyone of your justice and goodness, and
I will praise you all day long.　*Psalm 35:28*

In his goodness he chose to make us his own children
by giving us his true word. And we, out of all creation,
became his choice possession.　*James 1:18*

I will tell of the LORD's unfailing love. I will praise
the LORD for all he has done. I will rejoice in his great
goodness to Israel, which he has granted according to his
mercy and love.　*Isaiah 63:7*

YOU CAN SHOW YOUR APPRECIATION for God's goodness by telling others all that he has done for you and
by thanking him every day of your life.

God's Promise

Praise the LORD! Give thanks to the LORD, for he is
good! His faithful love endures forever.　*Psalm 106:1*

Faithfulness

What are the benefits of faithfulness?

God's Response

If we are faithful to the end . . . we will share in all that belongs to Christ.   *Hebrews 3:14*

You have been faithful with the little I entrusted to you, so you will be governor of ten cities as your reward. *Luke 19:17*

My servant Caleb is different from the others. He has remained loyal to me, and I will bring him into the land he explored. His descendants will receive their full share of that land.   *Numbers 14:24*

FAITHFULNESS BRINGS REWARDS in this life and for eternity. God is aware of the way that you approach life and is pleased when you are loyal to him. Others also recognize a woman's reputation for faithfulness and loyalty. Such a woman avoids trouble and gains security. The best reason to be faithful, however, is that God is faithful to you.

God's Promise

Remain faithful even when facing death, and I will give you the crown of life.   *Revelation 2:10*

Faithfulness

How do I develop faithfulness?

God's Response

Be faithful to the LORD your God as you have done until now. For the LORD has driven out great and powerful nations for you, and no one has yet been able to defeat you. Each one of you will put to flight a thousand of the enemy, for the LORD your God fights for you, just as he has promised. *Joshua 23:8-10*

No accounting was required from the construction supervisors, because they were honest and faithful workers. *2 Kings 12:15*

FAITHFULNESS IS LOYALTY, HONESTY, and commitment. Those who understand this are respected and trusted. You develop faithfulness by starting with the small things in life and working up to greater causes. Vow to be honest, committed, and faithful to the people in your life and to the work God has given you to do. Someday, when God greets you at heaven's door, he will say to you, "Well done, good and faithful servant."

God's Promise

He guards the paths of justice and protects those who are faithful to him. *Proverbs 2:8*

God's Faithfulness

How is God faithful?

God's Response

He is the Rock; his work is perfect. Everything he does is just and fair. He is a faithful God who does no wrong; how just and upright he is! *Deuteronomy 32:4*

God . . . always does just what he says, and he is the one who invited you into this wonderful friendship with his Son, Jesus Christ our Lord. *1 Corinthians 1:9*

Your unfailing love is higher than the heavens. Your faithfulness reaches to the clouds. *Psalm 108:4*

GOD ALWAYS DOES WHAT HE SAYS he will do. As you read the Bible, you will discover many promises from God that have already been fulfilled. This means that when you read the promises yet to come, you can count on God's faithfulness in fulfilling them. God is faithful to you because he promises that his love for you will never end. How faithful are you to God?

God's Promise

Give thanks to the LORD, for he is good! His faithful love endures forever. *1 Chronicles 16:34*

Gentleness

What does gentleness accomplish?
Won't everyone walk all over me if I am gentle?

God's Response

When the Holy Spirit controls our lives, he will produce this kind of fruit in us: love, joy, peace, patience, kindness, goodness, faithfulness, gentleness, and self-control. Here there is no conflict with the law.   *Galatians 5:22-23*

You should be known for the beauty that comes from within, the unfading beauty of a gentle and quiet spirit, which is so precious to God.   *1 Peter 3:4*

GENTLENESS DOES NOT MEAN that you are a doormat, letting others walk all over you. God is the perfect example of gentleness, and yet he is also a mighty warrior, able to defeat the powers of hell. In God's eyes, gentle people are the most powerful and influential in the world because they make an impact without a corresponding conflict or war. Gentleness may be the most powerful weapon in your arsenal. You accomplish more by gentleness than by coercion.

God's Promise

God blesses those who are gentle and lowly, for the whole earth will belong to them.   *Matthew 5:5*

God's Gentleness

How is God gentle?

God's Response

After the earthquake there was a fire, but the LORD was not in the fire. And after the fire there was the sound of a gentle whisper. . . . And a voice said, "What are you doing here, Elijah?" *1 Kings 19:12-13*

The LORD is like a father to his children, tender and compassionate to those who fear him. *Psalm 103:13*

GOD DOES NOT ALWAYS OPERATE on a spectacular scale. In fact, the spectacular does not always get our attention. Jesus' gentle words often made a greater impact upon people than his dramatic miracles. Sometimes your quiet and gentle words are just what a friend needs as an encouragement or a challenge. It is not always the loudest voice that is heard. The gentle quiet may be needed in order to hear what is really important. The next time you need to get a message across to someone, a gentle response in the midst of an uproar may be just what a person needs to hear.

God's Promise

You have given me the shield of your salvation. Your right hand supports me; your gentleness has made me great. *Psalm 18:35*

Gentleness

How did Jesus demonstrate gentleness?

God's Response

He will feed his flock like a shepherd. He will carry the lambs in his arms, holding them close to his heart. He will gently lead the mother sheep with their young. *Isaiah 40:11*

He felt great pity for the crowds that came, because their problems were so great and they didn't know where to go for help. *Matthew 9:36*

YOU SEE THE HEART OF JESUS best through images such as shepherding (holding you like a little lamb), having pity for crowds of hurting people, lifting heavy burdens, teaching us, giving us rest, and representing sinful people before almighty God. These are marks of gentleness.

God's Promise

Jesus said, "Come to me, all of you who are weary and carry heavy burdens, and I will give you rest. Take my yoke upon you. Let me teach you, because I am humble and gentle, and you will find rest for your souls." *Matthew 11:28-29*

Relationships

*How will gentleness make a difference
in my relationships?*

God's Response

A gentle answer turns away wrath, but harsh words stir up anger.   *Proverbs 15:1*

They must not speak evil of anyone, and they must avoid quarreling. Instead, they should be gentle and show true humility to everyone.   *Titus 3:2*

GENTLENESS STOPS QUARRELS, opens the door for forgiveness, and allows you to live and work with people graciously. That way, you can look beyond others' faults and appreciate the good qualities God has given them.

God's Promise

The wisdom that comes from heaven is first of all pure. It is also peace loving, gentle at all times, and willing to yield to others. It is full of mercy and good deeds. It shows no partiality and is always sincere.   *James 3:17*

Self-Control

What is self-control? Why is it necessary?

God's Response

When the Holy Spirit controls our lives, he will produce this kind of fruit in us: love, joy, peace . . . and self-control. *Galatians 5:22-23*

Spend your time and energy in training yourself for spiritual fitness. Physical exercise has some value, but spiritual exercise is much more important, for it promises a reward in both this life and the next. *1 Timothy 4:7-8*

SELF-CONTROL IS ONE OF THE HARDEST character traits to achieve, because it means denying what comes naturally to our sinful nature and replacing it with a controlled, godly response. Self-control is a lifelong endeavor, because just when you think you have one area of your life mastered, another area gets out of control. Some of the hardest things to control are our thoughts, our words, and our physical appetites. It is only with the help of the Holy Spirit that we achieve self-control. But when we do, we are pleasing to God and pleasing to others.

God's Challenge

It is better to have self-control than to conquer a city. *Proverbs 16:32*

Training

What are some steps to learning self-control?

God's Response

Keep me from deliberate sins! Don't let them control me. Then I will be free of guilt and innocent of great sin. *Psalm 19:13*

God wants you to be holy, so you should keep clear of all sexual sin. Then each of you will control your body and live in holiness and honor—not in lustful passion. *1 Thessalonians 4:3-5*

GOD WANTS US TO EXERCISE SELF-CONTROL over what we think, what we say, and what we do. He wants us to live as children of God, not as mindless followers of the godless ways of culture. We can do this by (1) honestly assessing our weaknesses; (2) determining that they will no longer rule us; (3) appealing to the Holy Spirit to help us stand strong against temptation; (4) humbly confessing to God when we make a mistake; and (5) giving glory to God when we are victorious!

God's Promise

All athletes practice strict self-control. They do it to win a prize that will fade away, but we do it for an eternal prize.   *1 Corinthians 9:25*

Words

How can I exercise control over my words?

God's Response

Take control of what I say, O LORD, and keep my lips sealed.   *Psalm 141:3*

I tell you . . . that you must give an account on judgment day for every idle word you speak.   *Matthew 12:36*

EXERCISING SELF-CONTROL OVER your words includes both what you shouldn't say and what you should say. For example, you shouldn't use profanity, complain, lie, or gossip. But you should speak up when you see injustice, you should encourage those who are down, and you should praise God every day. What comes out of your mouth most often? Ask a friend to make a mental list of your positive and negative words. If you really want to stop the negative words, ask yourself before you speak, "Is it true? Is it kind? Is it necessary?"

God's Promise

Don't use foul or abusive language. Let everything you say be good and helpful, so that your words will be an encouragement to those who hear them.   *Ephesians 4:29*

Gossip

Why is gossip so harmful?

God's Response

A gossip goes around revealing secrets, but those who are trustworthy can keep a confidence.   *Proverbs 11:13*

Gossip separates the best of friends.   *Proverbs 16:28*

What dainty morsels rumors are—but they sink deep into one's heart.   *Proverbs 18:8*

A gossip tells secrets, so don't hang around with someone who talks too much.   *Proverbs 20:19*

Others may accuse you of gossip. Then you will never regain your good reputation.   *Proverbs 25:10*

GOSSIP IS A SIN WE MUST AVOID. It unjustly robs another person of his or her reputation or uses someone else's information without their permission. Worse, gossip often does this with half-lies, half-truths, suggestions, and innuendos. Through gossip, we take away something precious that another person owns—their integrity. That may be the worst kind of theft.

God's Promise

Fire goes out for lack of fuel, and quarrels disappear when gossip stops.   *Proverbs 26:20*

Disconnection

What can happen if my life is not filled with the fruit of the Spirit?

God's Response

When you follow the desires of your sinful nature, your lives will produce these evil results: sexual immorality, impure thoughts, eagerness for lustful pleasure, idolatry, participation in demonic activities, hostility, quarreling, jealousy, outbursts of anger, selfish ambition, divisions, the feeling that everyone is wrong except those in your own little group, envy, drunkenness, wild parties, and other kinds of sin. . . . Anyone living that sort of life will not inherit the Kingdom of God. *Galatians 5:19-21*

THE HOLY SPIRIT CANNOT PRODUCE his fruit in your life if you aren't connected to the vine, Jesus Christ. If you're not connected, you are left to follow your sinful desires. How much better to remain in Christ and let him produce his fruit in you! Get reconnected. Pray, read your Bible, worship with other believers, and listen to God. Your life will be much happier.

God's Promise

I am the vine; you are the branches. Those who remain in me, and I in them, will produce much fruit. For apart from me you can do nothing. *John 15:5*

Temptation

Is it a sin to be tempted?

God's Response

The Devil came and said to him, "If you are the Son of God, change these stones into loaves of bread."

But Jesus told him, "No! The Scriptures say, 'People need more than bread for their life; they must feed on every word of God.'" *Matthew 4:3-4*

[Jesus] faced all of the same temptations we do, yet he did not sin. *Hebrews 4:15*

I**T IS NOT A SIN TO BE TEMPTED**—Jesus was tempted and he remained sinless. The fact that he faced temptation and never gave in to it means that he is able to understand and help you when you are tempted. Temptation is unavoidable, so when you are tempted, do what Jesus did—be ready to respond with the truth of Scripture. Knowing what is right according to God will help you resist sin.

God's Promise

Since he himself has gone through suffering and temptation, he is able to help us when we are being tempted. *Hebrews 2:18*

Danger

Why is temptation so dangerous?

God's Response

The fruit looked so fresh and delicious. . . . So she ate some.   *Genesis 3:6*

Temptation comes from the lure of our own evil desires. *James 1:14*

I am not surprised! Even Satan can disguise himself as an angel of light.   *2 Corinthians 11:14*

SATAN'S FAVORITE STRATEGIES ARE to make that which is sinful appear to be desirable and good, and to convince us that what is really false is true. He knows exactly how to confuse you. He knows you well enough to know your weaknesses. In fact, Satan is even now taking aim at the places where you are most vulnerable. Don't let Satan trick you with lies. Arm yourself with the truth God gives you in his Word.

God's Challenge

Keep alert and pray. Otherwise temptation will overpower you. For though the spirit is willing enough, the body is weak!   *Matthew 26:41*

Resisting Temptation

How can I resist temptation?

God's Response

Use every piece of God's armor to resist the enemy in the time of evil, so that after the battle you will still be standing firm. . . . Pray at all times and on every occasion in the power of the Holy Spirit. Stay alert and be persistent in your prayers for all Christians everywhere. *Ephesians 6:13, 18*

THE TIME TO PREPARE FOR BATTLE is before it begins. The time to prepare for temptation is before it overwhelms you. Your greatest defense against temptation is to arm yourself by praying and studying God's Word. Don't fool yourself into thinking that you can resist temptation without knowing the special tactics God provides in the Bible.

God's Promise

Remember that the temptations that come into your life are no different from what others experience. And God is faithful. He will keep the temptation from becoming so strong that you can't stand up against it. When you are tempted, he will show you a way out so that you will not give in to it.   *1 Corinthians 10:13*

Recovery

How do I recover after I have given in to temptation?

God's Response

My dear children, I am writing this to you so that you will not sin. But if you do sin, there is someone to plead for you before the Father. He is Jesus Christ, the one who pleases God completely. He is the sacrifice for our sins. He takes away not only our sins but the sins of all the world. . . . Those who say they live in God should live their lives as Christ did. *1 John 2:1-2, 6*

GOD'S GRACE IS GREATER than your failure. His forgiveness overcomes your sin. Satan only wins when he keeps you from turning back to God. No matter how often you fail, God welcomes you back through the love of Jesus Christ if you sincerely seek his forgiveness. Where else can you find that kind of forgiveness? Where else can you find that kind of love?

God's Promise

If we confess our sins to him, he is faithful and just to forgive us and to cleanse us from every wrong. *1 John 1:9*

Restoration

*How does God restore me to himself
after I have sinned?*

God's Response

"My wayward children," says the LORD, "come back to
me, and I will heal your wayward hearts." *Jeremiah 3:22*

"Come now, let us argue this out," says the LORD. "No
matter how deep the stain of your sins, I can remove it. I
can make you as clean as freshly fallen snow. Even if you
are stained as red as crimson, I can make you as white as
wool." *Isaiah 1:18*

G OD RESTORES YOU WHEN YOU confess your sins and
you are forgiven. After he forgives, he tramples
your sin under his feet, throws it into the ocean depths,
removes the stain, and makes you as clean as new snow.
He looks at you as though you had never sinned. God is
in the restoration business. He longs to heal your broken
heart and redeem your broken life.

God's Promise

The LORD says, "Then I will heal you of your idolatry
and faithlessness, and my love will know no bounds,
for my anger will be gone forever!" *Hosea 14:4*

Spiritual Warfare

Is spiritual warfare a reality?

God's Response

He said, "Don't be afraid, Daniel. Since the first day you began to pray for understanding and to humble yourself before your God, your request has been heard in heaven. I have come in answer to your prayer. But for twenty-one days the spirit prince of the kingdom of Persia blocked my way. Then Michael, one of the archangels, came to help me." *Daniel 10:12-13*

Jesus was led out into the wilderness by the Holy Spirit to be tempted there by the Devil. *Matthew 4:1*

THE BIBLE CLEARLY TEACHES that human beings are involved in a spiritual battle. Far from excluding you, faith puts you right in the middle of a spiritual battle for your very soul. You must recognize that and arm yourself, or you will be defeated.

God's Challenge

We are not fighting against people made of flesh and blood, but against the evil rulers and authorities of the unseen world, against those mighty powers of darkness who rule this world, and against wicked spirits in the heavenly realms. *Ephesians 6:12*

Spiritual Warfare

How does spiritual warfare affect me?

God's Response

Be careful! Watch out for attacks from the Devil, your great enemy. He prowls around like a roaring lion, looking for some victim to devour. Take a firm stand against him, and be strong in your faith.   *1 Peter 5:8-9*

THE PURPOSE OF EVIL IS TO DEFY GOD and to wear down believers until they are led into sin. This gives Satan pleasure and greater power over the earth. Therefore, you must be alert at all times for both the sneak attacks and the frontal attacks of the evil one. He will distort God's Word, hoping to make you doubt its integrity and, therefore, to question God's will and intentions for you. Eventually, God will destroy the power of evil for all time. Until that day, we overcome evil by choosing to obey God.

God's Challenge

Don't let anyone lead you astray with empty philosophy and high-sounding nonsense that come from human thinking and from the evil powers of this world, and not from Christ.   *Colossians 2:8*

Victory

*What does it mean to live the victorious
Christian life?*

God's Response

Every child of God defeats this evil world by trusting
Christ to give the victory.   *1 John 5:4*

Despite all these things, overwhelming victory is ours
through Christ, who loved us.   *Romans 8:37*

SIN ALWAYS DESTROYS—sometimes dramatically, sometimes slowly. Sin harasses you, constantly trying to
draw you away from your relationship with God. When
temptation is allowed to lurk around the edges of your
life, sin is allowed free reign in your heart. It is like a can-
cer that you fail to remove from your body. It is painful,
it infects you, and it will eventually kill you. The more
relentlessly you battle sin and remove it piece by piece
from your life, the more you will experience the victorious
Christian life and all its blessings. To achieve God's future
rewards, you must be obedient in the present.

God's Promise

How we thank God, who gives us victory over
sin and death through Jesus Christ our Lord!
1 Corinthians 15:57

Bad Habits

I could be victorious except for a few stubborn habits. How will God help me deal with bad habits?

God's Response

It seems to be a fact of life that when I want to do what is right, I inevitably do what is wrong. . . . Who will free me from this life that is dominated by sin? Thank God! The answer is in Jesus Christ our Lord. So you see how it is: In my mind I really want to obey God's law, but because of my sinful nature I am a slave to sin.   *Romans 7:21, 24-25*

ALTHOUGH OUR FINAL VICTORY over death through Christ is already assured, we must diligently apply that victory to the daily issues and temptations of life. We don't discipline ourselves in order to earn salvation, but to experience the joy and victory God intends for us now! You won't kick a bad habit overnight, but the surest way to change a bad habit is to replace it with a good one. With God's help, you can make progress every day. Today's victory is all you need for today—take it one day at a time.

God's Promise

Think clearly and exercise self-control. Look forward to the special blessings that will come to you at the return of Jesus Christ.   *1 Peter 1:13*

Good Habits

How can I develop good habits?

God's Response

Spend your time and energy in training yourself for spiritual fitness. Physical exercise has some value, but spiritual exercise is much more important.   *1 Timothy 4:7-8*

GOOD PHYSICAL HABITS—such as exercise, nutritious eating, and adequate rest—keep your body healthy and energetic. Godly habits—such as reading God's Word, praying, and giving your time and money in service—keep you spiritually healthy and energetic. Just as it takes time to kick a bad habit, so it takes time to develop a good one. The more you do it, the more natural it will become. Just as your body will become atrophied and sluggish without exercise and food, your spirit will dry up without a regular habit of meeting God every day through prayer and Bible reading. When you are spiritually shriveled, you can't enjoy the mercy and blessings that come from a relationship with God.

God's Promise

All athletes practice strict self-control. They do it to win a prize that will fade away, but we do it for an eternal prize.   *1 Corinthians 9:25*

Money

How can I develop good habits in handling my money?

God's Response

We didn't bring anything with us when we came into the world, and we certainly cannot carry anything with us when we die. So if we have enough food and clothing, let us be content. But people who long to be rich fall into temptation and are trapped by many foolish and harmful desires that plunge them into ruin and destruction. For the love of money is at the root of all kinds of evil. And some people, craving money, have wandered from the faith and pierced themselves with many sorrows.   *1 Timothy 6:7-10*

HOW YOU HANDLE YOUR MONEY REVEALS the condition of your soul. If Jesus asked you to, could you give up your house? Your car? Your lifestyle? Could you move to a crowded apartment in a poor neighborhood, ride the city buses, and never know where your next meal is coming from if that is how Jesus wants you to serve him? Your reaction may show whether money is your servant or your master. The best habit for handling money is to regularly test yourself by seeing how much of it you can give away.

God's Challenge

Trust in your money and down you go!   *Proverbs 11:28*

Money

What is a proper perspective toward money?

God's Response

No one can serve two masters. . . . You cannot serve both God and money.   *Matthew 6:24*

Stay away from the love of money; be satisfied with what you have. For God has said, "I will never fail you. I will never forsake you."   *Hebrews 13:5*

MONEY CAN BE VALUABLE IN HELPING to get God's work done on earth, so money itself is not evil—but the love of money can be. Money is dangerous when it deceives us into thinking that wealth will solve all of our problems. The love of money is sinful when we trust it, rather than God, for our security. Since God gave you the ability to make money, it really belongs to him. The crucial question is not how much of your money you should give to God, but how much of God's money you should keep.

God's Promise

Honor the LORD with your wealth and with the best part of everything your land produces. Then he will fill your barns with grain, and your vats will overflow with the finest wine.   *Proverbs 3:9-10*

Generosity

How much money should I give away?

God's Response

Bring all the tithes into the storehouse. . . . If you do, . . . I will open the windows of heaven for you. I will pour out a blessing so great you won't have enough room to take it in! Try it! Let me prove it to you! *Malachi 3:10*

You must each make up your own mind as to how much you should give. Don't give reluctantly or in response to pressure. For God loves the person who gives cheerfully. *2 Corinthians 9:7*

O LD TESTAMENT LAW MADE IT CLEAR that God wanted his people to tithe—to give him the first tenth of their income to demonstrate obedience and trust that he would provide for them. When Jesus came, he made it clear that he loves a cheerful giver. This means that he loves a generous heart. Whatever the amount, you should honor the Lord with your wealth so that his work on earth can boldly continue. God promises to bless us lavishly if we do this.

God's Promise

Whatever measure you use in giving—large or small— it will be used to measure what is given back to you. *Luke 6:38*

Debt

I've made some bad financial decisions.
Will God still help me deal with my debt?

God's Response

Don't worry about having enough food or drink or clothing. Why be like the pagans who are so deeply concerned about these things? Your heavenly Father already knows all your needs, and he will give you all you need from day to day if you live for him and make the Kingdom of God your primary concern. *Matthew 6:31-33*

YOU WILL HONOR GOD BY making a budget so that you live within your means and pay off your debt. God wants to help you be free of the burden of heavy debt because it makes you worry and distracts you from him. Ask God for wisdom. He knows your needs and will help you meet them if you are willing to make the necessary sacrifices.

God's Promise

"Bring all the tithes into the storehouse. . . . If you do," says the LORD Almighty, "I will open the windows of heaven for you. I will pour out a blessing so great you won't have enough room to take it in! Try it! Let me prove it to you!" *Malachi 3:10*

Panic

The worries in my life are causing me to panic.
How can I overcome these fears?

God's Response

Save me, O God, for the floodwaters are up to my neck.
Deeper and deeper I sink into the mire; I can't find a
foothold to stand on. . . . Turn and take care of me, for
your mercy is so plentiful.   *Psalm 69:1-2, 16*

As Pharaoh and his army approached . . . the people
began to panic, and they cried out to the LORD for help.
Then they turned against Moses and complained, "Why
did you bring us out here to die in the wilderness?"
Exodus 14:10-11

TOO OFTEN, A CRISIS EXPOSES our unbelief and fear
rather than our confidence and trust in God. Then
we panic. When that happens, stop and remember God's
faithfulness in the past. This will boost your faith in God
for deliverance from the present trial. Take your fears to
God. Reach out to him and grab hold. He won't let you go.

God's Promise

I have stilled and quieted myself, just as a small child is
quiet with its mother. Yes, like a small child is my soul
within me.   *Psalm 131:2*

Choices

Does God really care about my troubles—
even the ones I've brought on myself?

God's Response

I am waiting for you, O LORD. You must answer for me,
O Lord my God. . . . I am on the verge of collapse, facing
constant pain. But I confess my sins; I am deeply sorry for
what I have done.   *Psalm 38:15, 17-18*

GOD OFTEN ALLOWS THE CONSEQUENCES of sin to run
their course—even for believers—precisely because
he cares about them. God uses consequences to remind
you of the danger of sin, to encourage you to work hard to
avoid it, and to prepare you to face even stronger temptations in the future. He cares for you so deeply that he will
even use your self-made troubles to discipline you. It is
better to suffer from God's gentle discipline than to let
temptation pull us away from God.

God's Promise

"In those days when you pray, I will listen. If you look for
me in earnest, you will find me when you seek me. I will
be found by you," says the LORD.   *Jeremiah 29:12-14*

Staying Strong

How can I stay strong in times of trouble?

God's Response

You can be sure of this: The LORD has set apart the godly for himself. The LORD will answer when I call to him. *Psalm 4:3*

Listen to my voice in the morning, LORD. Each morning I bring my requests to you and wait expectantly. *Psalm 5:3*

YOU FIND OUT WHERE YOUR faith stands when trouble comes. Are you really able to put your trust completely in God, or do you accuse him and become angry with him? You can stay strong if you learn to look at these times as God's way of drawing you closer to him. You will feel closest to God during times of trouble because that is when you will cling to him. He is always there, waiting to answer when you call.

God's Promise

If we endure hardship, we will reign with him. If we deny him, he will deny us. *2 Timothy 2:12*

Perseverance

Why is it important that I learn to persevere?

God's Response

Because he bends down and listens, I will pray as long as I have breath!   *Psalm 116:2*

We can rejoice, too, when we run into problems and trials, for we know that they are good for us—they help us learn to endure. And endurance develops strength of character in us, and character strengthens our confident expectation of salvation.   *Romans 5:3-4*

TO STAY STRONG, TO PERSEVERE, TO ENDURE—these characteristics help you to deal with problems. You know that when you persevere through difficult times, God is developing strength of character in you. God uses adversity to make you strong. Without adversity, there is nothing to exercise your faith. Ask God to give you a glimpse of what he wants you to learn as you persevere through difficult times.

God's Promise

Everyone will hate you because of your allegiance to me. But those who endure to the end will be saved.
Matthew 10:22

Heroes

Most heroes are those who persevere against hardship. How can I emulate such people?

God's Response

All of these people we have mentioned received God's approval because of their faith, yet none of them received all that God had promised. For God had far better things in mind for us that would also benefit them, for they can't receive the prize at the end of the race until we finish the race. *Hebrews 11:39-40*

GOD'S HEROES ARE THOSE WHO HANG ON to their faith in him no matter what happens. The Bible is full of examples of people who never stopped trusting God even though they were mocked, persecuted, or killed for their faith. God may not ask you to be a martyr for him, but is your faith strong enough to endure even a little derision or scorn? Determine to be faithful to God no matter what.

God's Promise

We give great honor to those who endure under suffering. Job is an example of a man who endured patiently. From his experience we see how the Lord's plan finally ended in good, for he is full of tenderness and mercy. *James 5:11*

Endurance

In what areas should I develop endurance?

God's Response

These are the laws and regulations you must obey as long as you live in the land the LORD, the God of your ancestors, is giving you.   *Deuteronomy 12:1*

You have patiently suffered for me without quitting. *Revelation 2:3*

They encouraged them to continue in the faith, reminding them that they must enter into the Kingdom of God through many tribulations.   *Acts 14:22*

WHEN YOU CONTINUE TO obey God's Word even in difficult times, you demonstrate that your faith is strong. When you refuse to get discouraged and give up, God promises great rewards. Trusting God means that you always confidently expect him to be present to guide you through each day until you see him face-to-face when you enter his heavenly Kingdom.

God's Promise

Don't get tired of doing what is good. Don't get discouraged and give up, for we will reap a harvest of blessing at the appropriate time.   *Galatians 6:9*

Vision

How do I obtain good spiritual vision?

God's Response

The people's minds were hardened. . . . A veil covers their minds so they cannot understand the truth. And this veil can be removed only by believing in Christ. *2 Corinthians 3:14*

Elisha prayed, "O LORD, open his eyes and let him see!" The LORD opened his servant's eyes, and when he looked up, he saw that the hillside around Elisha was filled with horses and chariots of fire. *2 Kings 6:17*

IT SEEMS IRONIC THAT THE ONLY WAY for some of us to see better is to cover our eyes with glass lenses. With spiritual vision, you need the lens of faith—the ability to believe that there is much more happening than you can see. When you face difficulties that seem insurmountable, remember that spiritual armies are fighting for your soul. Open your spiritual eyes to view God's power.

God's Promise

Be silent, and know that I am God! I will be honored by every nation. I will be honored throughout the world. *Psalm 46:10*

Good News

Why is it important for me to tell others about Jesus?

God's Response

How can they call on him to save them unless they believe in him? And how can they believe in him if they have never heard about him? And how can they hear about him unless someone tells them? And how will anyone go and tell them without being sent? That is what the Scriptures mean when they say, "How beautiful are the feet of those who bring good news!"   *Romans 10:14-15*

GOD HAS GIVEN HIS PEOPLE the privilege and responsibility of telling others about him. You should share the Good News about Jesus with delight and enthusiasm because it is not just Good News, but the Greatest News. Hearing it or not is literally a life-and-death matter. The only way some will hear is if you tell them, just as someone told you!

God's Challenge

Go into all the world and preach the Good News to everyone, everywhere.   *Mark 16:15*

Sharing Your Faith

How will God help me share my faith?

God's Response

When the Holy Spirit has come upon you, you will receive power and will tell people about me everywhere—in Jerusalem, throughout Judea, in Samaria, and to the ends of the earth.   *Acts 1:8*

We cannot stop telling about the wonderful things we have seen and heard.   *Acts 4:20*

Jesus called out to them, "Come, be my disciples, and I will show you how to fish for people!"   *Mark 1:17*

WHEN YOU STEP OUT IN FAITH, the Holy Spirit will give you power, words, and direction. You can prepare yourself by thinking about how you would describe your faith to someone who doesn't understand it. What would you tell someone who asked about your faith?

God's Promise

Now go, and do as I have told you. I will help you speak well, and I will tell you what to say.   *Exodus 4:12*

Witness

What should my witness include?

God's Response

I decided to concentrate only on Jesus Christ and his death on the cross. *1 Corinthians 2:2*

If you confess with your mouth that Jesus is Lord and believe in your heart that God raised him from the dead, you will be saved. *Romans 10:9*

We testify and announce to you that he is the one who is eternal life. *1 John 1:2*

THE BEST WAY TO WITNESS IS to tell your own faith story. No one can argue with that. Tell people how God has touched your life and how he continues to do so each day. Some might scoff or make fun of you, but many people are starving for truth and love and will be open to what you have to say. God will give you the words. Don't be afraid to ask someone if they are ready to have Jesus in their life.

God's Challenge

If you are asked about your Christian hope, always be ready to explain it. But you must do this in a gentle and respectful way. *1 Peter 3:15-16*

Planting

What do I do when people aren't interested in hearing about Christ?

God's Response

My job was to plant the seed in your hearts, and Apollos watered it, but it was God, not we, who made it grow. *1 Corinthians 3:6*

When they heard Paul speak of the resurrection of a person who had been dead, some laughed, but others said, "We want to hear more about this later." That ended Paul's discussion with them, but some joined him and became believers. *Acts 17:32-34*

You must give them my messages whether they listen or not. *Ezekiel 2:7*

SOMETIMES YOUR ROLE IS SIMPLY to plant a seed. You can't make people believe; only the Holy Spirit can soften their hearts and make them ready. Your job is simply to tell them and let God do the rest.

God's Promise

You know that the way we lived among you was further proof of the truth of our message. *1 Thessalonians 1:5*

Trustworthiness

How can I earn the trust that will help people listen to me when I share my faith?

God's Response

After David had finished talking with Saul, he met Jonathan, the king's son. There was an immediate bond of love between them, and they became the best of friends. From that day on Saul kept David with him at the palace and wouldn't let him return home. And Jonathan made a special vow to be David's friend. *1 Samuel 18:1-3*

You have been faithful with the little I entrusted to you, so you will be governor of ten cities as your reward. *Luke 19:17*

YOU EARN TRUST SIMPLY by being trustworthy, beginning with the small things. When people know they can depend on you, they will more readily listen to what you say. It has been said that we need to tell people about Christ, and if necessary, we should use words! Let your witness begin with your character and actions.

God's Challenge

Put away all falsehood and "tell your neighbor the truth" because we belong to each other. *Ephesians 4:25*

Trust

How can I avoid trusting in the wrong people or the wrong things?

God's Response

Trust in the LORD with all your heart; do not depend on your own understanding. Seek his will in all you do, and he will direct your paths.   *Proverbs 3:5-6*

Without consulting me, you have gone down to Egypt to find help. You have put your trust in Pharaoh for his protection. But in trusting Pharaoh, you will be humiliated and disgraced.   *Isaiah 30:2-3*

THE WRONG THINGS IN LIFE often seem attractive to the human heart and mind, making us gullible. That is why it is so important to weigh what you hear, using God's Word as the standard of truth. It is also wise to seek advice from godly people who follow the Lord closely. Then you won't worry about following the wrong people or things.

God's Promise

It is better to trust the LORD than to put confidence in people. It is better to trust the LORD than to put confidence in princes.   *Psalm 118:8-9*

Salt and Light

How can I help people understand their need to trust in God?

God's Response

Let your good deeds shine out for all to see, so that everyone will praise your heavenly Father.   *Matthew 5:16*

Jesus shouted to the crowds, "If you trust me, you are really trusting God who sent me. For when you see me, you are seeing the one who sent me. I have come as a light to shine in this dark world, so that all who put their trust in me will no longer remain in the darkness."   *John 12:44-46*

YOU CAN'T MAKE PEOPLE TRUST IN GOD, but you can facilitate the process if you faithfully reflect Jesus' love. When others see the love of Jesus in you, many will want to know what makes you so different. People will be attracted to a beacon of light that offers hope for a safe journey in a dark world. When they come to you because of the light of Jesus, use Jesus' words to tell them about their need for God.

God's Promise

I trust in your unfailing love. I will rejoice because you have rescued me. I will sing to the LORD because he has been so good to me.   *Psalm 13:5-6*

Giving Thanks

Why is it important for me to give thanks to the Lord?

God's Response

Giving thanks is a sacrifice that truly honors me. If you keep to my path, I will reveal to you the salvation of God. *Psalm 50:23*

All of your works will thank you, LORD, and your faithful followers will bless you.   *Psalm 145:10*

Since everything God created is good, we should not reject any of it. We may receive it gladly, with thankful hearts.   *1 Timothy 4:4*

THANKING GOD SHOWS AN ATTITUDE of gratitude. A thankful heart honors God for what he has done and recognizes his work, mercy, provision, and blessing in your life. A thankful heart gives you a positive attitude because it keeps you focused on all God is doing for you, not on what you think you lack. Make giving thanks a part of your prayer time, and thank God for something every day.

God's Promise

Since we are receiving a kingdom that cannot be destroyed, let us be thankful and please God by worshiping him with holy fear and awe. *Hebrews 12:28*

Thankfulness

How can I show my thankfulness to the Lord?

God's Response

I will thank you, LORD, with all my heart; I will tell of all the marvelous things you have done.   *Psalm 9:1*

It is good to give thanks to the LORD, to sing praises to the Most High. It is good to proclaim your unfailing love in the morning, your faithfulness in the evening. *Psalm 92:1-2*

When I learn your righteous laws, I will thank you by living as I should!   *Psalm 119:7*

THERE ARE MANY WAYS TO SHOW your thankfulness to the Lord—through praise, prayer, singing, worship, giving, obedience, and serving. Like you, God loves to hear a simple thank-you.

God's Promise

Give thanks to the LORD and proclaim his greatness. Let the whole world know what he has done.
1 Chronicles 16:8

Thankfulness

What should I thank God for?

God's Response

I will thank the LORD with all my heart as I meet with his godly people. How amazing are the deeds of the LORD! All who delight in him should ponder them.   *Psalm 111:1-2*

I will give thanks to your name for your unfailing love and faithfulness, because your promises are backed by all the honor of your name.   *Psalm 138:2*

Give thanks to the LORD, for he is good!   *Psalm 118:1*

Thank God for his Son—a gift too wonderful for words!
2 Corinthians 9:15

THERE ARE SO MANY THINGS to thank God for—
salvation, faith, heaven, miracles, food, other believers, family, work, nature, laughter, his unfailing love and faithfulness, his honor, his goodness, his Son . . . in fact, you can give thanks for everything!

God's Promise

You will always give thanks for everything to God the Father in the name of our Lord Jesus Christ.
Ephesians 5:20

Thankfulness

How can I show my thankfulness to others?

God's Response

"Oh, thank you, sir!" she exclaimed.   *1 Samuel 1:18*

He fell face down on the ground at Jesus' feet, thanking him for what he had done. This man was a Samaritan. *Luke 17:16*

THERE ARE MANY WAYS TO SHOW your thankfulness to others—a word of thanks, a smile, a note, a meal, a gift, a prayer, a recommendation. To whom can you say thank you today?

God's Promise

I have never stopped thanking God for you. I pray for you constantly, asking God, the glorious Father of our Lord Jesus Christ, to give you spiritual wisdom and understanding, so that you might grow in your knowledge of God.   *Ephesians 1:16-17*

Thankfulness

How can I be thankful even in the tough times?

God's Response

Don't worry about anything; instead, pray about everything. Tell God what you need, and thank him for all he has done.   *Philippians 4:6*

No matter what happens, always be thankful, for this is God's will for you who belong to Christ Jesus. *1 Thessalonians 5:18*

WE MAY NOT FEEL THANKFUL for the tough times, but we can be thankful in them. How we look at our problems determines our outlook on life. If we see them only as problems, we will usually develop an attitude of bitterness, cynicism, and hopelessness. If we see them as a crucible for strengthening our character and convictions, then we are better able to rise above them, and even thank God for how they are refining our lives.

God's Promise

Since we are his children, we will share his treasures— for everything God gives to his Son, Christ, is ours, too. But if we are to share his glory, we must also share his suffering. Yet what we suffer now is nothing compared to the glory he will give us later.   *Romans 8:17-18*

Purification

Why do tough times come? What value do they have in my life?

God's Response

Fire tests the purity of silver and gold, but the LORD tests the heart.   *Proverbs 17:3*

Remove the dross from silver, and the sterling will be ready for the silversmith.   *Proverbs 25:4*

I will bring that group through the fire and make them pure, just as gold and silver are refined and purified by fire. They will call on my name, and I will answer them. I will say, "These are my people," and they will say, "The LORD is our God."   *Zechariah 13:9*

AS PRECIOUS METALS ARE REFINED BY FIRE, so your life, which is precious to God, is refined and purified in the fire of adversity. It is only through refining that the impurities are removed. When the liquid metal is completely purified, the refiner's image appears on its surface. Likewise, through suffering, God's image will appear more and more clearly in you.

God's Challenge

He will sit and judge like a refiner of silver, watching closely as the dross is burned away.   *Malachi 3:3*

Trouble

How can I avoid trouble?

God's Response

Blessed are those who have a tender conscience, but the stubborn are headed for serious trouble.   *Proverbs 28:14*

The trustworthy will get a rich reward. But the person who wants to get rich quick will only get into trouble. *Proverbs 28:20*

Here on earth you will have many trials and sorrows. But take heart, because I have overcome the world.   *John 16:33*

THERE ARE TWO KINDS OF TROUBLE—that which you cause because of a mistake, a bad decision, or an act of sin, and trouble that invades your life through no fault of your own. The first kind of trouble can usually be avoided through good planning and godly living. The second kind usually cannot be avoided, but God promises to help us through it and to eliminate it forever one day. You won't always be able to avoid trouble, but you can keep from looking for it!

God's Promise

The power of the life-giving Spirit has freed you through Christ Jesus from the power of sin that leads to death. *Romans 8:2*

Grace

What is grace?

God's Response

The wages of sin is death, but the free gift of God is eternal life through Christ Jesus our Lord.   *Romans 6:23*

God saved you by his special favor when you believed. And you can't take credit for this; it is a gift from God. Salvation is not a reward for the good things we have done, so none of us can boast about it.   *Ephesians 2:8-9*

GRACE IS BOTH A ONETIME ACT (the grace of God in giving you salvation through faith in Jesus) and a way of life (allowing the grace of God to continue to do wonderful works in you). In either case, grace is simply God's special favor. Because of his grace, God gives you many things that you don't deserve and can't take credit for. When you understand God's grace, you will want to be a person of grace to those around you.

God's Promise

All of these things are for your benefit. And as God's grace brings more and more people to Christ, there will be great thanksgiving, and God will receive more and more glory.   *2 Corinthians 4:15*

Grace

How does God's grace make a difference in my life?

God's Response

Sin is no longer your master, for you are no longer subject to the law, which enslaves you to sin. Instead, you are free by God's grace.   *Romans 6:14*

I am not one of those who treats the grace of God as meaningless. For if we could be saved by keeping the law, then there was no need for Christ to die.   *Galatians 2:21*

If you are trying to make yourselves right with God by keeping the law, you have been cut off from Christ! You have fallen away from God's grace.   *Galatians 5:4*

GOD'S GRACE MAKES ALL THE difference in your life. It is the difference between belonging to God or being alone, between having strength or being weak, between being free or a slave to sin, between enjoying God's friendship or being his enemy, between heaven or hell! Imagine a life without God's grace, and you imagine a life of loneliness, fear, slavery, guilt, weakness, and helplessness. Thank God that he has bestowed his grace on you.

God's Promise

By God's grace, Jesus tasted death for everyone in all the world.   *Hebrews 2:9*

Grace

How should God's grace affect my view of him?

God's Response

The LORD is merciful and gracious; he is slow to get angry and full of unfailing love.   *Psalm 103:8*

Rejoice in the LORD your God! For the rains he sends are an expression of his grace. Once more the autumn rains will come, as well as the rains of spring.   *Joel 2:23*

USING GOD'S RIGHTEOUSNESS as the standard, we must conclude that every one of us stands guilty before him. In a very real sense, we've committed treason against the King by disobeying his law and rebelling against him. We deserve judgment, a life sentence. Instead, God offers us forgiveness and freedom to live in his Kingdom forever. This is a God who is slow to get angry and full of love. This is a God who wants to show us mercy instead of judgment. When you view God as loving and kind rather than mean and vindictive, your whole perspective changes on how he affects your life.

God's Promise

Let us come boldly to the throne of our gracious God. There we will receive his mercy, and we will find grace to help us when we need it.   *Hebrews 4:16*

Mercy

What is the difference between God's justice, mercy, and grace?

God's Response

The dead were judged according to the things written in the books, according to what they had done. *Revelation 20:12*

The LORD is merciful and gracious; he is slow to get angry and full of unfailing love. He will not constantly accuse us, nor remain angry forever. He has not punished us for all our sins, nor does he deal with us as we deserve. *Psalm 103:8-10*

God saved you by his special favor when you believed. And you can't take credit for this; it is a gift from God. Salvation is not a reward for the good things we have done, so none of us can boast about it.   *Ephesians 2:8-9*

JUSTICE WOULD GIVE US what we deserve. Mercy holds back from giving us what we deserve. Grace gives us what we do not deserve.

God's Promise

The unfailing love of the LORD never ends! By his mercies we have been kept from complete destruction. *Lamentations 3:22*

Mercy

How does God show mercy?

God's Response

When Lot still hesitated, the angels seized his hand and the hands of his wife and two daughters and rushed them to safety outside the city, for the LORD was merciful. *Genesis 19:16*

The LORD your God is merciful—he will not abandon you or destroy you or forget the solemn covenant he made with your ancestors. *Deuteronomy 4:31*

God is so rich in mercy, and he loved us so very much, that even while we were dead because of our sins, he gave us life when he raised Christ from the dead. *Ephesians 2:4-5*

G OD SHOWERS MERCY ON YOU EACH DAY. He is slow to get angry over your sins, he offers you a way out from the eternal consequences of sin, and he shows you unfailing love no matter what you have done.

God's Promise

He saved us, not because of the good things we did, but because of his mercy. *Titus 3:5*

Priceless Gifts

As I enter this busy season, what are some priceless gifts I should be thinking about?

God's Response

Come and show me your mercy, as you do for all who love your name.   *Psalm 119:132*

May the grace of the Lord Jesus Christ be with your spirit. *Philippians 4:23*

GOD'S GRACE AND MERCY CAN be constant reminders of what is really important. As you begin the holiday season, ask God to help you focus on who he is and what he has done for you. Ask him to make his grace and mercy real to you each day. As you escape what you deserve, and as you receive what you don't deserve, offer this same mercy and grace to those around you. These are the most priceless gifts you can give.

God's Promise

May grace, mercy, and peace, which come from God our Father and from Jesus Christ his Son, be with us who live in truth and love.   *2 John 1:3*

Emptiness

I know this is a wonderful season of the year, but I feel so empty. How can I fill that emptiness?

God's Response

In the few days of our empty lives, who knows how our days can best be spent? And who can tell what will happen in the future after we are gone?　*Ecclesiastes 6:12*

Jesus replied, "People soon become thirsty again after drinking this water. But the water I give them takes away thirst altogether. It becomes a perpetual spring within them, giving them eternal life."　*John 4:13-14*

B Y NOW YOU MAY ALREADY be overly busy with extra shopping, baking, and decorating. You may do a lot and accomplish much, but after a while it all feels empty and meaningless if there is no lasting purpose behind what you do. A heart without God is an empty heart. Don't confuse accomplishment with purpose. During this coming Christmas season, focus on the reason for it. The Christ child who came wants to fill your heart with real meaning and purpose.

God's Promise

You know that God paid a ransom to save you from the empty life you inherited.　*1 Peter 1:18*

Loneliness

I'm feeling alone. How can God help me?

God's Response

I alone am left.   *1 Kings 19:10*

He went in alone and shut the door behind him and prayed to the LORD.   *2 Kings 4:33*

How precious are your thoughts about me, O God! They are innumerable!   *Psalm 139:17*

YOU MAY FEEL ALONE, but God is always with you. He is thinking about you all the time. Don't give up on God when you are lonely. This will cause you to feel sorry for yourself and become discouraged. Use this "alone time" to focus on God. You may also be helped by connecting with other people. Getting involved with others will take your focus off yourself and you'll feel less alone. Put yourself in places where you can meet and get to know people. Soon your life will be full and blessed with friendship.

God's Promise

Don't be afraid, for I am with you. Do not be dismayed, for I am your God. I will strengthen you. I will help you. I will uphold you with my victorious right hand. *Isaiah 41:10*

Belonging

How can I be sure that I belong to God?

God's Response

How can we be sure that we belong to him? By obeying his commandments. If someone says, "I belong to God," but doesn't obey God's commandments, that person is a liar and does not live in the truth. But those who obey God's word really do love him. That is the way to know whether or not we live in him.   *1 John 2:3-5*

OBEYING GOD IS A REFLECTION of your love for him and your belief in him. Since you are human, you cannot obey God perfectly all of the time. God is looking for sincere motives—the desire always to please and obey him. King David committed adultery, had a man murdered, and lied, yet God called him a "man after my own heart" (Acts 13:22). This was because David, more than perhaps any person who ever lived, desperately wanted to obey God because he loved God so much. When you have that desire, you know that you belong to him.

God's Promise

Yet I still belong to you; you are holding my right hand.
Psalm 73:23

Stress

I know I'm God's child, so why do I feel so stressed out?

God's Response

Jesus said, "Let's get away from the crowds for a while and rest." There were so many people coming and going that Jesus and his apostles didn't even have time to eat. *Mark 6:31*

Jesus said, "Come to me, all of you who are weary and carry heavy burdens, and I will give you rest." *Matthew 11:28*

STRESS IS A REALITY IN LIFE. Sometimes stress is good— it can motivate you to get going. At other times, stress is bad and can cause any number of mental and physical problems. If you're feeling stressed out over the holiday season, you may need to take a breather or get away for a few hours. Refresh yourself with a nap, a little time spent on a hobby, an hour of meditation in your favorite chair, a chat with a friend, or time reading God's Word.

God's Promise

Don't get tired of doing what is good. Don't get discouraged and give up, for we will reap a harvest of blessing at the appropriate time. *Galatians 6:9*

Burnout

What should I do if I'm experiencing burnout?

God's Response

When Moses' father-in-law saw all that Moses was doing for the people, he said, "Why are you trying to do all this alone? . . . You're going to wear yourself out—and the people, too. This job is too heavy a burden for you to handle all by yourself." *Exodus 18:14, 18*

YOU MAY BE EXPERIENCING BURNOUT if you become unusually weak and exhausted in the middle of doing your work, or if you feel constantly overwhelmed. Sometimes you feel burned out at the end of a project or a great personal victory. When you are stretched in every direction for too long a time, you lose focus and can't do anything well. You can reach this point quickly during the holidays, when you try to make Christmas look like everything that tradition says it should! To enjoy the spirit of Christmas, you will need to pause. Adequate sleep, good nourishment, and asking for help will refresh you so you can truly enjoy the season.

God's Promise

He gives power to those who are tired and worn out; he offers strength to the weak. *Isaiah 40:29*

Boundaries

I know I can avoid burnout if I set some boundaries for myself. But how do I do that?

God's Response

Our goal is to stay within the boundaries of God's plan for us. *2 Corinthians 10:13*

GOD GIVES US VERY CLEAR BOUNDARIES for living the Christian life. These are not meant to keep us from having fun; they're meant to protect us. The same principle applies to our normal, everyday lives. Without boundaries, chaos reigns, we get burned out, and we suffer. To avoid burnout in this busy season, you must set some boundaries. Start by making a list of what you must do and what you'd like to do. Then start scratching things off your list until you feel you will have enough time to enjoy your family and the joy of the season. Freeing yourself from the trap of incessant activity requires asking for help and learning to say no—even to worthwhile activities.

God's Promise

There is a time for everything, a season for every activity under heaven. *Ecclesiastes 3:1*

Coping

How can I cope when life's demands seem overwhelming?

God's Response

As I looked at everything I had worked so hard to accomplish, it was all so meaningless.   *Ecclesiastes 2:11*

Martha was worrying over the big dinner she was preparing. . . . But the Lord said to her, "My dear Martha, you are so upset over all these details! There is really only one thing worth being concerned about. Mary has discovered it—and I won't take it away from her."   *Luke 10:40-42*

THE KEY TO COPING IS to set your priorities early. Don't let everyone else decide what your day should look like—that should be between you and God. If you make time with him your first priority of the day, you will find that he will give you perspective on your activities for the rest of the day. Ask God to show you what is worth being concerned about.

God's Promise

As for God, his way is perfect. All the LORD's promises prove true. He is a shield for all who look to him for protection.   *2 Samuel 22:31*

Coping

How do I cope when others fail me or hurt me?

God's Response

Stop putting your trust in mere humans. They are as frail as breath. How can they be of help to anyone?   *Isaiah 2:22*

We are hunted down, but God never abandons us. *2 Corinthians 4:9*

PEOPLE HAVE THE CAPACITY to hurt one another—and it happens all the time. The potential for hurting each other can increase during the holidays, as people are extra busy and stressed. Even beloved friends and family can get on your nerves at this time of year. During these stressful days, everyone needs an extra measure of grace, strength, and peace of mind. God promises to supply those without hurting your feelings. If you want a friend who will never fail you, trust the One who will always love you. This doesn't mean that you should distrust everyone else, especially family and friends who are usually trustworthy. But understand that even people who love you will disappoint you. That makes God's faithfulness even sweeter.

God's Promise

Jesus said, "Father, forgive them, for they don't know what they are doing."   *Luke 23:34 (NLT2)*

God's Presence

With all of my faults and failures, how can I enter God's presence?

God's Response

No matter how deep the stain of your sins, I can remove it. I can make you as clean as freshly fallen snow.   *Isaiah 1:18*

Now all of us, both Jews and Gentiles, may come to the Father through the same Holy Spirit because of what Christ has done for us.   *Ephesians 2:18*

Because of our faith, Christ has brought us into this place of highest privilege where we now stand, and we confidently and joyfully look forward to sharing God's glory.   *Romans 5:2*

WHEN YOU ACCEPT JESUS as Lord of your life, he forgives you and purifies you so that he can live in you. When Jesus purifies you, he cleanses your heart and makes it as clean and fresh as new snow. He leaves no stains! Your faults and failures are gone as far as he is concerned, so enter his presence with joy!

God's Promise

If we are living in the light of God's presence, just as Christ is, then we have fellowship with each other, and the blood of Jesus, his Son, cleanses us from every sin.   *1 John 1:7*

God's Presence

How is God "with me" and "in me"?

God's Response

The Lord himself will choose the sign. Look! The virgin will conceive a child! She will give birth to a son and will call him Immanuel—"God is with us." *Isaiah 7:14*

GOD CAME TO BE "WITH US" when he sent his Son as a baby to live in a human body, to live a perfect life, and to suffer and die in order to save us from sin. His resurrection conquered death and sin, after which he sent his Holy Spirit to remain with you and in you. The God of the universe devised this plan from the beginning of time, knowing that you would need him to save you and live in you. During this season, celebrate the birth of Jesus with the knowledge that God's plan, set in motion by the birth of a baby, was designed especially for you.

God's Promise

He is the Holy Spirit, who leads into all truth. The world at large cannot receive him, because it isn't looking for him and doesn't recognize him. But you do, because he lives with you now and later will be in you. *John 14:17*

Connection

What happens when I stay connected to Jesus?

God's Response

Yes, I am the vine; you are the branches. Those who remain in me, and I in them, will produce much fruit. For apart from me you can do nothing.   *John 15:5*

WHEN YOU ARE CONNECTED TO JESUS, he turns your simple acts into something profound and purposeful. For example, he turns your simple act of singing into a profound chorus of praise that ministers to an entire congregation. He turns your simple act of placing your tithe in the offering plate into a profound act of mercy that will touch the heart of the needy person who receives it. He turns your simple act of teaching children in Sunday school into a profound moment in the heart of a child who suddenly realizes the need for salvation. Stay connected to Jesus and let him turn your simple acts of service into profound works for the Kingdom of God.

God's Promise

Glory be to God! By his mighty power at work within us, he is able to accomplish infinitely more than we would ever dare to ask or hope.   *Ephesians 3:20*

Perseverance

Sometimes I feel too weak to hang on; will God hang on to me?

God's Response

Because you trusted me, I will preserve your life and keep you safe. I, the LORD, have spoken!   *Jeremiah 39:18*

He will keep you strong right up to the end, and he will keep you free from all blame on the great day when our Lord Jesus Christ returns.   *1 Corinthians 1:8*

I am sure that God, who began the good work within you, will continue his work until it is finally finished on that day when Christ Jesus comes back again.   *Philippians 1:6*

TEN DAYS AWAY FROM CHRISTMAS! By now, you are either eager to celebrate or in despair over all that still needs to be done. Now is the time to rely on the Lord for extra strength and endurance. He will preserve you, steady you, keep you strong, and continue to work in you—not only until Christmas, but until the day he returns to earth.

God's Promise

All glory to God, who is able to keep you from stumbling, and who will bring you into his glorious presence innocent of sin and with great joy.   *Jude 1:24*

DECEMBER 16   Unto Us a Child Is Born

Why was Jesus' birth so special?

God's Response

A child is born to us, a son is given to us. The government will rest on his shoulders. And he will be called: Wonderful Counselor, Mighty God, Everlasting Father, Prince of Peace. *Isaiah 9:6 (NLT2)*

I bring you good news that will bring great joy to all people. The Savior—yes, the Messiah, the Lord—has been born today in Bethlehem. *Luke 2:10-11 (NLT2)*

THERE IS NOTHING AS JOYOUS as the birth of a baby. Family and friends wait nine long months to meet the new person. The little bundle of joy changes your life forever from the first time you meet. He or she is so sweet, so full of potential. Jesus' birth was all that and more. Not only friends and family, but all generations since the beginning of time had been waiting for the birth of this child. Even nature proclaimed his birth. The potential he held was the salvation of all people. He changes your life as soon as you meet him, not only here on earth, but for eternity.

God's Promise

God did not send his Son into the world to condemn it, but to save it. *John 3:17*

A Son Is Given

*Why did God have to give his Son
as a sacrifice for us?*

God's Response

A child is born to us, a son is given to us.   *Isaiah 9:6*

God so loved the world that he gave his only Son, so that everyone who believes in him will not perish but have eternal life.   *John 3:16*

I F YOU ARE A PARENT, you know you would do anything for your child's welfare, even to the point of death. To save your child's life, you would gladly give up yours. Yet God did the unthinkable—he gave up his only child! He purposely and willingly sent Jesus to earth to live as a human, and to experience the same joy and pain that we do. But then he was tortured and crucified and punished for our sins so we wouldn't have to experience that. Could you make such a sacrifice? That is the ultimate sacrifice of love. Don't let such lavish love be wasted. Accept God's gift of salvation and embrace the Christ child with all your heart.

God's Promise

God showed how much he loved us by sending his only Son into the world so that we might have eternal life through him. This is real love.   *1 John 4:9-10*

The Government Will Rest on His Shoulders

Can I rest on Jesus' shoulders?

God's Response

A child is born to us, a son is given to us. And the government will rest on his shoulders.   *Isaiah 9:6*

Yet it was our weaknesses he carried. . . . The LORD laid on him the sins of us all.   *Isaiah 53:4, 6 (NLT2)*

AT CHRISTMAS, when we celebrate the birth of Jesus, we don't usually think about the hard part of the story. But the little baby Jesus grew into a man who shouldered the sins of the world. His shoulders were beaten and whipped bloody, they bore a cross up a hill, and then they hung on that cross until his death cleared away our guilt for sin. Just as Jesus bore our sins on his shoulders, he now carries our burdens. In fact, our future for eternity rests on them. Jesus invites you now to rest on him. Let him carry you. He's strong enough to bear any troubles you have—after all, he has carried the weight of the world.

God's Promise

I will be your God throughout your lifetime—until your hair is white with age. I made you, and I will care for you. I will carry you along and save you.   *Isaiah 46:4*

Wonderful Counselor

How is Jesus my Counselor?

God's Response

A child is born to us, a son is given to us. . . . And he will be called: Wonderful Counselor.   *Isaiah 9:6 (NLT2)*

True wisdom and power are with God; counsel and understanding are his.   *Job 12:13*

"Who can know what the Lord is thinking? Who can give him counsel?" But we can understand these things, for we have the mind of Christ.   *1 Corinthians 2:16*

IF YOU ARE FORTUNATE, you have someone in your life on whom you can always depend for advice. You are blessed when that person is not only wise and godly but loving and caring as well—and always willing to give you as much time as you need. Jesus is such a counselor. He came for the purpose of giving you loving, caring, perfect counsel. He will carry you through life and into eternity.

God's Promise

I will send you the Counselor—the Spirit of truth. He will come to you from the Father and will tell you all about me.   *John 15:26*

Mighty God

How can a tiny baby be the mighty God?

God's Response

A child is born to us, a son is given to us. . . . And he will be called . . . Mighty God.   *Isaiah 9:6 (NLT2)*

Suddenly, a terrible storm came up. . . . Jesus . . . stood up and rebuked the wind and waves, and suddenly all was calm. The disciples just sat there in awe. "Who is this?" they asked themselves. "Even the wind and waves obey him!"   *Matthew 8:24, 26-27*

I depend on Christ's mighty power that works within me. *Colossians 1:29*

I T'S HARD TO PICTURE THE BABY JESUS as almighty God. But he was mighty enough to create the world, live a sinless life, heal countless people, calm storms, and conquer death. He's mighty enough to conquer your troubles, too!

God's Promise

By his mighty power at work within us, he is able to accomplish infinitely more than we would ever dare to ask or hope.   *Ephesians 3:20*

Everlasting Father

How is God my father?

God's Response

A child is born to us, a son is given to us. . . . And he will be called . . . Everlasting Father.   *Isaiah 9:6 (NLT2)*

His name is the LORD—rejoice in his presence! Father to the fatherless, defender of widows.   *Psalm 68:4-5*

I will be your Father, and you will be my sons and daughters, says the Lord Almighty.   *2 Corinthians 6:18*

A GOOD FATHER SHOWS HIS LOVE for his children by spending time with them, providing for them, protecting them, celebrating with them, disciplining them, praying with them, teaching them right from wrong, and leading them to faith in Jesus Christ. God is the perfect father, and he always will be. Earthly fathers sometimes let you down, and eventually they leave this earth, but God will never disappoint you, and his love is everlasting. He longs to "father" you. Go to his strong, loving arms for your security.

God's Promise

The LORD is like a father to his children, tender and compassionate to those who fear him.   *Psalm 103:13*

Prince of Peace

How does Jesus bring peace into my life?

God's Response

A child is born to us, a son is given to us. . . . And he will be called . . . Prince of Peace. *Isaiah 9:6 (NLT2)*

Don't be troubled. You trust God, now trust in me. . . . I am going to prepare a place for you. . . . When everything is ready, I will come and get you, so that you will always be with me where I am. *John 14:1-3*

THERE ARE SO MANY THINGS THAT affect peace: chaos, conflict, interruptions, wars, busyness, worry, fear. On this earth, you can't prevent many of these things, but you can have peace—a quiet, unshakable confidence—about the outcome. Some people have great peace just before they are martyred for their faith in Jesus because they know where they are going. In the same way, you can know that *you* are going to live forever with the Lord in perfect peace. Let that assurance keep you from panicking in today's storms. The outcome is certain.

God's Promise

Here on earth you will have many trials and sorrows. But take heart, because I have overcome the world. *John 16:33*

Jesus' Birth

Why was Jesus' birth so different?

God's Response

The Savior . . . has been born today in Bethlehem. . . . And you will recognize him by this sign: You will find a baby wrapped snugly in strips of cloth, lying in a manger. *Luke 2:11-12 (NLT2)*

Remember, dear brothers and sisters, that few of you were wise in the world's eyes, or powerful, or wealthy when God called you. *1 Corinthians 1:26*

GOD OFTEN ACCOMPLISHES his purposes in unexpected ways. God used the census of a heathen emperor to bring Joseph and Mary to Bethlehem. Maybe that is also why he chose to have Jesus born in a stable rather than a palace, why he chose Bethlehem rather than Jerusalem, and why the news of Jesus' birth went first to shepherds rather than to kings. God may have done all this to show that life's greatest treasure—salvation through Jesus— is available to all. It may also show that the lowly and humble have a better chance of receiving that message.

God's Promise

God blesses those who are humble, for they will inherit the whole earth. *Matthew 5:5 (NLT2)*

Incarnation

Why did God send his Son into the world as a baby?

God's Response

God in his gracious kindness declares us not guilty. He has done this through Christ Jesus, who has freed us by taking away our sins.   *Romans 3:24*

GOD'S MISSION WAS TO SAVE US for eternity and to show us how to live. The Incarnation (the Son of God coming to us "in the flesh") means that God, in the form of a human baby, entered into our world to identify with our situation, to experience our suffering, and to suffer for our salvation. We can never claim that God doesn't understand us because God truly stood where we stand. Refusing to stand aloof or apart from us, the Lord entered fully into our lives (see Hebrews 2:14-18). As one of us, yet as one who is also fully divine, he was able to pay the full price for our sin, thus opening the way to eternal life. But he is also able to show how to live in surrender and obedience to God (see John 14:15-21).

God's Promise

God so loved the world that he gave his only Son, so that everyone who believes in him will not perish but have eternal life.   *John 3:16*

Responding to Jesus

What should our response be to Jesus?

God's Response

They entered the house and saw the child . . . and they bowed down and worshiped him.   *Matthew 2:11 (NLT2)*

We praise God for the wonderful kindness he has poured out on us because we belong to his dearly loved Son. *Ephesians 1:6*

"My Lord and my God!" Thomas exclaimed.   *John 20:28*

THE ASTROLOGERS TRAVELED THOUSANDS of miles to see the king of the Jews. When they finally found him, they responded with joy, worship, and gifts. How different from the approach we often take today! We expect God to come looking for us, explain himself, prove who he is, and give us gifts. Those who are wise still seek Jesus because he is unlike any other person and he was sent for a special purpose. Do you really know who he is? What gift can you give back to Jesus, who gave his life for you?

God's Promise

Look! Here I stand at the door and knock. If you hear me calling and open the door, I will come in, and we will share a meal as friends.   *Revelation 3:20*

Reflection

How can I keep Christmas alive all year long?

God's Response

Mary quietly treasured these things in her heart and thought about them often.   *Luke 2:19*

Praise the LORD, I tell myself, and never forget the good things he does for me.   *Psalm 103:2*

CHRISTMAS IS OVER, and all the secrets are out. The gifts have been opened, the feast devoured, the songs sung, the joy celebrated. Today is a good day to take some time to reflect, as Mary did over two thousand years ago, on the events of the big day, on the gifts that were given, and on the love bestowed. Store the good times and memories in your heart to be thought about and smiled over in the weeks and months ahead. Reflect on the goodness of God, who gave the best gift of all—his Son.

God's Promise

We will not hide these truths from our children but will tell the next generation about the glorious deeds of the LORD. We will tell of his power and the mighty miracles he did.   *Psalm 78:4*

Regrets

As this year ends, I have some regrets.
How do I deal with them?

God's Response

I focus on this one thing: Forgetting the past and looking forward to what lies ahead, I press on to reach the end of the race and receive the heavenly prize for which God, through Christ Jesus, is calling us.   *Philippians 3:13-14 (NLT2)*

What this means is that those who become Christians become new persons. . . . The old life is gone. A new life has begun!   *2 Corinthians 5:17*

A S YOU APPROACH THE END OF THE YEAR, it's natural to look back and reflect on different events. Some memories bring smiles, but others bring regrets. Now is a good time to clean house, that is, to confess to God what needs to be confessed, apologize and make amends to those you have wronged, and then leave the pain behind. Forget the failures of the past and move forward into the new year with expectation and excitement.

God's Promise

If we confess our sins to him, he is faithful and just to forgive us and to cleanse us from every wrong.
1 John 1:9

Finishing Well

How can I plan to finish well next year?

God's Response

The master was full of praise. "Well done, my good and faithful servant. You have been faithful in handling this small amount, so now I will give you many more responsibilities. Let's celebrate together!"   *Matthew 25:21*

Hezekiah encouraged the Levites for the skill they displayed as they served the LORD.   *2 Chronicles 30:22*

I T'S ALMOST SCARY WHEN another year has slipped by. You wonder where it went and how it went by so quickly. That's why it's so important to do your best each day—in your work, in your relationships, in your walk with God, and yes, even in your rest. Be faithful to the responsibilities and the call God has given you. Then, at year's end, you will have the satisfaction of a job well done, and God will be pleased.

God's Promise

I am sure that God, who began the good work within you, will continue his work until it is finally finished on that day when Christ Jesus comes back again.
Philippians 1:6

Plans

What must I do to prepare for the coming year?

God's Response

"I know the plans I have for you," says the LORD. "They are plans for good and not for disaster, to give you a future and a hope." *Jeremiah 29:11*

Trust in the LORD with all your heart; do not depend on your own understanding. Seek his will in all you do, and he will direct your paths. *Proverbs 3:5-6*

The LORD says, "I will guide you along the best pathway for your life. I will advise you and watch over you." *Psalm 32:8*

GOD ALREADY KNOWS WHAT THE NEXT YEAR will hold for you. He has some great plans for you. He will advise you as you go and watch over you along the way. When you have asked for God's guidance and direction, you can move forward with confidence, knowing that his purpose and work will be accomplished.

God's Promise

We know that God causes everything to work together for the good of those who love God and are called according to his purpose for them. *Romans 8:28*

New Creation

*How can I ensure that I will be better off
a year from now?*

God's Response

He died for everyone so that those who receive his new life
will no longer live to please themselves. Instead, they will
live to please Christ, who died and was raised for them.
2 Corinthians 5:15

Look at those who are honest and good, for a wonderful
future lies before those who love peace. *Psalm 37:37*

THERE'S A WHOLE NEW YEAR just around the corner. It's
a fresh start, with no mistakes made yet. In a sense,
this is the chance to become a new person. In the year
ahead, commit to growing every day in your relationship
with the Lord, even just a little bit. Ask the Holy Spirit to
change you, day by day, into all God wants you to be. If
you grow closer to God, you will be better off.

God's Promise

Those who become Christians become new persons.
They are not the same anymore, for the old life is gone.
A new life has begun! *2 Corinthians 5:17*

What should I stop doing, and what should I start doing in order to begin the year well and end it well?

God's Response

Stop loving this evil world and all that it offers you.
1 John 2:15

I pray that you will begin to understand the incredible greatness of his power for us who believe him.
Ephesians 1:19

STOP LOOKING BACK. Stop thinking you can't overcome a bad habit or addiction. Stop thinking God doesn't care. Stop blaming yourself or others. Stop doing what you know you should not do. Start each day with God in prayer and Bible reading. Start showing more grace and forgiveness. Start a good habit. Start committing more random acts of kindness. Start obeying God's Word. This is a good time to commit to stopping and starting and to remember that God is the one constant that will never change all year. He loves you and will always be at your side.

God's Promise

May the LORD bless you and protect you. May the LORD smile on you and be gracious to you. May the LORD show you his favor and give you his peace.   *Numbers 6:24-26*

Index